EDUCATION
OF A
WANDERING MAN

G·K
Hall
&Co.

Also published in Large Print
from G.K. Hall by Louis L'Amour:

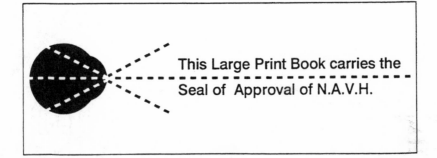

This Large Print Book carries the
Seal of Approval of N.A.V.H.

EDUCATION
OF A
WANDERING MAN

Louis L'Amour

G.K. Hall & Co.
Thorndike, Maine

Published in Large Print by arrangement with Bantam Books, a
division of Bantam Doubleday Dell Publishing Group, Inc.,
New York, New York.

G.K. Hall Large Print Book Series.

Set in 16 pt. News Plantin.

Printed on acid free paper in the United States of America.

Library of Congress Cataloging-in-Publication Data

L'Amour, Louis, 1908-1988
    Education of a wandering man / Louis L'Amour.
       p. cm.
    ISBN 0-8161-5797-9 (alk. paper : lg. print)
    1. L'Amour, Louis, 1908-1988—Biography.
    2. Novelists, American—20th century—Biography.
    3. Large type books. I. Title.
    [PS3523.A446Z464 1993]
    813'.52—dc20   93-1971
                                                      CIP

To Alberto and Gioia Vitale

INTRODUCTION
Joys of Random Reading

by Daniel J. Boorstin

We are often told that we are what we eat. In our world since the printing press it might be more accurate to say we are what we read. How each of us digests what we read is a mystery. And what people really read is sometimes as puzzling as what they really think.

This book tells a surprising tale of the reading of the beloved best-selling writer Louis L'Amour. For his shaping wandering years were years of reading. When he left school in the tenth grade he began an earnest self-education stirred by a passion for books. These early working and wandering years, which took him around the world, were filled with days and nights of reading. And with books happily encountered on shipboard or in the cabin of a mining camp, in Sumatra or on the China coast.

He was a lone reader but somehow never felt lonely in the company of a book. This account of his reading reminds us that little of it was done in the company of other readers, or fellow students, or with the promise, which we enjoy in settled literary company, of a lively bookish conversation. He must have been an especially vigorous self-starter and an imaginative self-rewarder.

There are quite a few surprises here for those who have only read his books but did not have the good fortune to know the lovable man himself. Anyone who visited Louis in his spacious study with its sixteen-foot-high ceiling with walls of specially designed bookshelves will not be surprised. For the bookshelves that Louis designed were much like the man himself. Each tall row of shelves made a kind of book-covered door that could be swung open to reveal another sixteen-foot set of book-filled shelves fixed to the wall behind. Louis was a modest man, slow to reveal what he really knew.

While many of us are tempted to pretend to have read what we think we should have read, Louis was not that way. For most of us Mark Twain's definition of a classic — "a book which people praise and don't read" — is accurate enough. But certainly not for Louis. In conversation he was frequently reaching for the name of the author of that book that told him something which might interest you too. Louis had a prodigious memory, which usually brought up the full correct name of the author, the title of the work, how many volumes of it there were, and often even the date of publication. Many of his vivid memories were of multivolume works like Gibbon's *Decline and Fall of the Roman Empire* or Sansom's *History of Japan*.

Not a gourmet reader, Louis was blessed with an insatiable literary appetite. He had a natural preference for books that had stood the test of time. His memory was so well stocked that he delighted in returning to browse in books that were rich in association with where he had first met them. He explains here that he does not write about sex because it is only "a leisure activity" while "I am writing about men and women who were settling a new country, finding their way through a maze of difficulties, and learning to survive despite them." Although this kindly man found it hard to express distaste or lack of sympathy for anybody, he was troubled by what seemed to him the sexual obsessions and aberrations of our time. An indefatigable, skilled storyteller, he delighted in the broad effervescent currents of experience, he remained untinged by the ambiguities of much that he read, and he kept his own values undented.

Perhaps one reason why his book-memories were so vivid was that once his early "yondering years" were over, he traveled abroad very little. Still, he remained an avid reader. Jealous of any time not used for writing, he luxuriated within his walls of books. His remarkable memory left him little need to refresh himself about details. As he writes in this volume, he could call up exotic places he had visited or read about without revisiting. But for three weeks each summer he would reexplore with his family some Western lands, probably as much for love of the landscape as for any other reason. He had seen and done so much during those early years chronicled here that we can understand why he might have feared that another trip would be anticlimactic, or even dull some sharp early memories.

A few years ago when I was at work on *The Discoverers* and trying to learn about Marco Polo, among others, I told Louis what I was about. At the time he was working on *The Walking Drum* and he came up at once with an astonishingly fluent and accurate critical bibliography — on the strengths and weaknesses of Yule's edition of the Travels and of the later books on Marco Polo. Then I had the pleasure of seeing his ample, well-thumbed collection of Marco Poliana neatly shelved on the walls of his study.

Still, as this volume reveals, Louis was anything but a systematic reader. A spectacularly serendipitous reader, he enlists us in the joys of random reading — from Schliermacher's *Soliloquies*, Boswell's *Johnson*, Bertrand Russell's *Marriage and Morals*, Eric Hoffer's *True Believer*, Gregg's *Commerce of the Prairies* to Roger Baldwin's *Liberty under the Soviets* — with an occasional dip into George Santayana, Joseph Conrad, and Rabindranath Tagore and some frolics by the way in Baudelaire's poems, Claude McKaye's *Harlem Shadows*, Frank Dobie's *Longhorns*, Polybius' histories, and Voltaire's *Candide*. Good, bad, or indifferent, fiction or nonfiction, classic or ephemera — all were grist for his mill! But unlike many self-educated men and other good storytellers,

Louis was a good listener, as eager to learn from the spoken as from the printed word.

Obviously there are advantages to programmed reading that cannot be secured in any other way. Louis, by force of circumstances and from a passion for books, sought and found other advantages. He enjoyed and was stirred by countless unprogrammed juxtapositions — the fate of the Incas and of the Roman Empire, Shakespeare's sonnets, Jack London's tales and Plato's dialogues. He could quote Robert W. Service and William Butler Yeats, Rudyard Kipling and Percy Bysshe Shelley and Oscar Wilde in the same breath. For he was utterly without intellectual snobbery or cultural pretensions.

So Louis never worried about whether a book "fitted in" to his reading program. To be a book gave it dignity enough — a claim on his time and attention, and on his patience for the author's weaknesses.

The love of books made him — like any other lover — sometimes excessively charitable to his authors. And this, too, made him rare among copious readers. In this volume you will find enthusiasm, excitement, and gratitude to the whole miscellany of authors ancient and modern, East and West. That was Louis's way — to find or squeeze something of value from every printed page.

He was lucky in his times. It happened that the 1930s, which he chronicles in this volume, was an especially fertile time for American publishing — F. N. Doubleday, Max Schuster, Alfred Knopf, Bennett Cerf, among others, not to mention the Haldeman Julius little blueback books and the Modern Library. The Book-of-the-Month Club and The Literary Guild and others were disseminating good books in new ways, the Great Books were filtering down. It was an age of serious best sellers, a good age for desultory reading.

Louis gives us a lesson — too seldom offered by academic or professional critics — in open-mindedness and literary charity. And he encourages us, too, to become Wandering Readers, joining his search for the joys and surprises in the pages of books.

1

It was May 14. In a few days my class back in Jamestown, North Dakota would be graduating from high school, and I was in Singapore.

The date is one of the few I know from those knockabout years, simply because I had the good sense to write it on the inside cover of a book I bought at the shop of Muhammed Dulfakir on the corner of High Street. The book was Kipling's *Departmental Ditties*, and my reason for buying it was that I had forgotten a line or two from a poem I liked to recite, "The Ballad of Fisher's Boarding House."

During those years I often recited poetry in bunkhouses in mining or lumber camps, and in ship's fo'c'sles. It was usually the verse of Robert W. Service or Rudyard Kipling, but there was a lot of poetry floating around written for, and often by, the kind of men we were, occasionally printed but usually passed from memory to memory.

On that day several of my shipmates had gathered around a table or two in the Maypole Bar, a place no doubt long forgotten. Such men as "Hans, the blue-eyed Dane" of Kipling's poem would have known it, and probably British soldiers stationed in town. It was a nondescript bar, convenient to the waterfront.

This is not the story of how I came to be in Singapore. That will be told elsewhere. This is a story of an adventure in education, pursued not under the best of conditions. The idea of education has been so tied to schools, universities, and professors that many assume there is no other way, but education is available to anyone within reach of a library, a post office, or even a newsstand.

Today you can buy the *Dialogues* of Plato for less than you would spend on a fifth of whiskey, or Gibbon's *Decline and Fall of the Roman Empire* for the price of a cheap shirt. You can buy a fair beginning of an education in any bookstore with a good stock of paperback books for less than you would spend on a week's supply of gasoline.

Often I hear people say they do not have time to read. That's absolute nonsense. In the one year during which I kept that kind of record, I read twenty-five books while waiting for people. In offices, applying for jobs, waiting to see a dentist, waiting in a restaurant for friends, many such places. I read on buses, trains, and planes. If one really wants to learn, one has to decide what is important. Spending an evening on the town? Attending a ball game? Or learning something that can be with you your life long?

Byron's *Don Juan* I read on an Arab dhow sailing north from Aden up the Red Sea to Port Tewfik on the Suez Canal. Boswell's *Life of Samuel Johnson* I read while broke and on the beach in San Pedro. In Singapore, I came upon a copy of *The Annals* and *Antiquities of Rajahstan* by James Tod. It was in the library of a sort of YMCA for seamen, the name of which I've forgotten but which any British sailor of the time would remember, for the British had established them in many ports, for sailors ashore.

At that time I could no more than skim the James Tod book, reading only a few chapters before I was off to sea again. But a few years ago I located a secondhand copy in a bookstore in Greenwich Village and it now rests on a shelf in my own library, a source for several planned books.

A great book begins with an idea; a great life, with a determination.

My life may not be great to others, but to me it has been one of steady progression, never dull, often exciting, often hungry, tired, and lonely, but always learning. Somewhere back down the years I decided, or my nature decided for me, that I would be a teller of stories.

Decisions had to be made and there was nobody but me to make them. My course altered a number of times but never deviated from the destination I had decided upon. Whether this was altogether a matter of choice I do not know. Perhaps my early reading and the storytelling at home had preconditioned me for the role I adopted.

Somewhere along the line I had fallen in love with learning, and it became a lifelong romance. Early on I discovered it was fun to follow along the byways of history to find those treasures that await any searcher. It may be that all later decisions followed naturally from that first one.

One thing has always been true: That book or that person who can give me an idea or a new slant on an old idea is my friend.

And there have been many such.

Right here I wish to say that what follows is not an autobiography, although no doubt these materials are a piece of the final picture, which I hope to undertake later.

As can be guessed from the title, this book is about education, but not education in the accepted sense. No man or woman has a greater appreciation for schools than I, although few have spent less time in them. No matter how much I admire our schools, I know that no university exists that can provide an education; what a university can provide is an outline, to give the learner a direction and guidance. The rest one has to do for oneself.

If I were asked what education should give, I would say it should offer breadth of view, ease of understanding, tolerance for others, and a background from which the mind can explore in any direction.

Education should provide the tools for a widening and deepening of life, for increased appreciation of all one sees or experiences. It should equip a person to live life well, to understand what is happening about him, for to live life well one must live with awareness.

No one can "get" an education, for of necessity education is a continuing process. If it does nothing else, it should provide students with the tools for learning, acquaint them with methods of study and research, methods of pursuing an idea. We can only hope they come upon an idea they wish to pursue.

In the United States we have concentrated tremendous sums of money on the educational plant, seemingly with the idea that the right number of buildings will turn out the right number of graduates. Yet the teachers who actually instruct the future citizens of our country are more often than not miserably paid. If in the future we find ourselves with a lot of fourth-rate citizens, we have only ourselves to blame.

Education depends on the quality of the teacher, not the site or beauty of the buildings — nor, I might add, does it depend on the winning record of the football team, and I like football.

It is constantly reiterated that education begins in the home, as indeed it does, but what is often forgotten is that morality begins in the home also.

It also begins in the car seat, where many a budding criminal career is born when the child not only watches his parent repeatedly break traffic laws, but hears him lie about it when caught. The example is not, supposedly, expected to influence the child.

My own education, which is the one I know most about, has been haphazard, a hit-and-miss affair that was and continues to be thoroughly delightful.

I came into the world with two priceless advantages: good health and a love of learning. When

I left school at the age of fifteen I was halfway through the tenth grade. I left for two reasons, economic necessity being the first of them. More important was that school was interfering with my education.

Due to circumstances, it was essential that I go to work and try to support myself. This was no sacrifice, for it had been uppermost in my mind for some time. Several factors contributed to my discontent.

My first job was as messenger boy for the Western Union, a good job for a boy in my hometown. I got the job when I was twelve, and it was in the telegraph office that I first began to type. I cannot say that I *learned* to type — I began with two fingers and work with them still. It has been called the hunt-and-peck system, but over the years my fingers have become so used to the typewriter that I hunt very little and peck a lot.

Also, I was growing rapidly. At twelve I was the size of most other boys; at thirteen and a half I was my present height, which is six feet and one inch. The very effort of growing left me often tired. Through the first six grades my own grades were good, always at the top or close to the top. As a matter of fact, I was usually second, third, or fourth in the class, except in math. In my sixth grade, where we had a teacher who loved math, I several times made an A, or what corresponded to it.

Moving into the seventh grade, I discovered I had several compulsory subjects in which I considered myself qualified, at least to the extent provided by the school text. It was essential that I take a semester of ancient history, and I had already done much reading in the area.

I wished to skip the subject and take modern history, of which I knew very little. I also wished to skip general science and take chemistry. At the time I had helped build several crystal radio sets and had done some electroplating. At the library I had read from books on botany and geology.

Actually, the book on general science I read in the city library was much better, as well as much more interesting, than the school text, but the rules made no provisions for exceptions. I did not look forward to spending time studying subjects already covered.

Ours was a family in which everybody was constantly reading, and where literature, politics, history, and the events of the prize ring were discussed at breakfast, lunch, and dinner. We grew up with the names of H. G. Wells, George Bernard Shaw, John L. Sullivan, Bob Fitzsimmons, and Jack Dempsey as familiar to us as those of our own family, right along with Teddy Roosevelt, William Howard Taft, Woodrow Wilson, Sitting Bull, and Crazy Horse.

The Apache wars of which I was to write later occurred far away to the southwest, but the Sioux were close by. They had killed and scalped my own great-grandfather while he was with the Sibley command, pursuing the Santee Sioux out across Dakota in the aftermath of the bloody Little

Crow massacre of 1862.

My education in domestic and foreign affairs began at home. My sister Edna was attending Jamestown College, and my two older brothers and a second sister were in school, constantly discussing and arguing about schoolwork, reciting poetry, and talking of books they were reading.

How many books we had in our home I do not remember, and doubt if anyone ever counted. We had collections of Longfellow, Whittier, Lowell, and Emerson, as well as the Stoddard lectures on travel. All of us had library cards, and they were always in use. Reading was as natural to us as breathing.

When I moved on from children's books and fairy tales, one of the first books I read was Robert Louis Stevenson's *Treasure Island*.

I had begun reading earlier than most, because my sister Emmy Lou, no doubt to keep me from bothering her, decided it was easier to teach me to read stories to myself rather than to read them to me, as she had been doing.

What books I read immediately after that, or their progression, I do not remember, but certainly they were for a time the simplest of children's books. I do know that when I was in the fifth grade my father told me he would give me a three-volume *History of the World* if I would read it. The books had come as a premium with a subscription to *Collier's* magazine, if I recall correctly. For the next few months, when my father came home I would sit on his knee and tell him what I had read during the day.

The books had a buff binding, a good many pictures, and fairly large print, so they must have been very general indeed.

Other books remembered from those years were *Black Beauty*, a similar book about a dog called *Beautiful Joe* (who was not beautiful at all), *Little Lord Fauntleroy*, *Pilgrim's Progress* (which I found very dull), *John Halifax, Gentleman*, and two old favorites, *Cudjo's Cave* and *The Little Shepherd of Kingdom Come*.

My older brothers had left behind a dozen Horatio Alger novels, which I read, but I remember only three titles: *Brave and Bold*, *Do and Dare*, and *Jed, the Poorhouse Boy*.

About the same time, I read at least a dozen novels by G. A. Henty, a British author. The only two recalled offhand were *The Lion of the North*, about Gustavus Adolphus of Sweden, and *With Clive in India*. Aside from teaching much more about aspects of history studied in school, they provided at least a passing familiarity with events our schools did not touch upon. These deepened my interest in history and brought not questions but rather a desire to know more about what actually happened and why.

Historical novels are, without question, the best way of teaching history, for they offer the human stories behind the events and leave the reader with a desire to know more. Due to such books, and later reading, I found that no matter what country I visited or whom I met, I knew something of the history or romance of the country, or about a person's homeland.

My father, who was a veterinarian working mostly with horses and cattle, was a great story-teller. In small towns in those days nearly every public official had some other business, and my father was at various times a deputy sheriff, a policeman, a Juvenile Commissioner, and for many years was alderman of the First Ward, the largest in the city. At one time he even ran for mayor but was defeated by a good friend.

He told stories of his boyhood in the lumber woods, of a pet bear and deer he owned, of a Huron Indian boy with whom he played. My mother, too, told stories, usually of her relatives in Minnesota or of her father, a veteran of the Civil and Indian Wars who lived with us when I was very small.

Supposedly I was too young to remember him well, but often when we were alone he drew diagrams on a slate and told me how the great battles of history were fought, and about some of his own wars. I should not have remembered, but years later I could draw a diagram of how the Battle of Cannae was won, and I did not study that until later.

2

Before that day in Singapore I had skinned dead cattle in Texas, baled hay in New Mexico, worked as a roustabout with the Hagenbeck-Wallace Circus, and in between times had boxed a couple of exhibitions in small towns and won a few fights. I had hoboed across Texas on the Southern Pacific and shipped out to the West Indies as a seaman and, later, on another ship, to Liverpool and Manchester, England. Returning, I had planted fruit trees near Phoenix, worked as caretaker of a mine in the Bradshaws, and spent three very rough months "on the beach" in San Pedro.

Riding a freight train out of El Paso, I had my first contact with the Little Blue Books. Another hobo was reading one, and when he finished he gave it to me.

The Little Blue Books were a godsend to wandering men and no doubt to many others. Published in Girard, Kansas, by Haldeman-Julius, they were slightly larger than a playing card and had sky-blue paper covers with heavy black print titles. I believe there were something more than three thousand titles in all and they were sold on newsstands for 5 or 10 cents each. Often in the years following, I carried ten or fifteen of them in my pockets, reading when I could.

Among the books available were the plays of Shakespeare, collections of short stories by De Maupassant, Poe, Jack London, Gogol, Gorky, Kipling, Gautier, Henry James, and Balzac. There were collections of essays by Voltaire, Emerson, and Charles Lamb, among others.

There were books on the history of music and architecture, painting, the principles of electricity; and, generally speaking, the books offered a wide range of literature and ideas. I do not recall exactly, but I believe the first Blue Book given me on that freight train was Robert Louis Stevenson's *Dr. Jekyll and Mr. Hyde.*

In subsequent years I read several hundred of the Little Blue Books, including books by Tom Paine, Charles Darwin, and Thomas Huxley.

To properly understand the situation in America before the Depression, one must realize there was a great demand for seasonal labor, and much of this was supplied by men called hoboes.

Over the years the terms applied to wanderers have been confused until all meaning has been lost. To begin with, a bum was a local man who did not want to work. A tramp was a wanderer of the same kind, but a hobo was a wandering worker and essential to the nation's economy.

In the days before the big combines it was the hobo who "shocked" the grain, picking up the bundles dropped by a binder and stacking them to be picked up by men on hayracks.

Many hoboes would start working the harvest

in Texas and follow the ripening grain north through Oklahoma, Kansas, and Nebraska into the Dakotas. During harvest season, when the demand for farm labor was great, the freight trains permitted the hoboes to ride, as the railroads were to ship the harvested grain and it was in their interest to see that labor was provided.

Often this lot of wandering workers was mixed with college boys earning enough money for school or working to get in shape for football. Some simply drifted because they enjoyed the life, the work in the open fields, the variety of towns and experiences, and the chance to see the country. By and large these harvest workers were Anglo-Saxon and Irish, as most of the early pioneers had been, but there was a good mixture of blacks and immigrants of European extraction. Latinos were rarely seen except in the southwestern states.

The Depression brought a different kind of drifter to the railroads and highways, and only one who bridged that period can grasp the depth of the change. The Depression hoboes had little of that carefree, cheerful attitude of the earlier hobo. They were serious, often frightened men. They had come from towns where work was no longer available, and were, as we all were, seeking work. Often these men had families to whom they wrote when they could afford the postage.

The criminal element in either segment was small indeed. The fact of the matter is that poor men do not often steal, and when they do, it is petty theft, something to eat or perhaps an item of clothing to keep them from the cold.

Thieves are usually those who have something and want more. They steal not for food but for flashier clothes, a better watch, a handsome car. They steal for money to spend on flash, on women or drugs. Hungry men are without power, without leverage, and so are vulnerable to any kind of bullying and are constantly suspected of crimes they rarely commit.

The years before the Depression were the heyday of the hobo. His labor was much in demand and he, loving to wander, rarely stayed long on a job. For years there had been a surplus of labor in the United States, but it was largely unrecognized because so many were constantly shifting jobs. There were at least four or five men for every job, but with the constant turnover, some of them were working all the time; when the Depression came it was like a game of musical chairs. Those who had the jobs stayed with them, while the others were left adrift in a country without work.

During the knockabout years the hobo acquired a literature of his own, stories, poetry, and songs passed on by word of mouth, only occasionally printed or recorded. Among the songs best remembered, although there were hundreds now lost, were "Hallelujah, I'm a Bum," "The Bum Song," "The Dying Hobo," "Big Rock Candy Mountain," and "The Hype Song."

The folklore of the hobo has been studied but only partly explored, and is extensive indeed. The chapters on famous hoboes, tramps, and railroad

26

detectives have been largely overlooked because too few of the old hoboes are left, and those who know the old stories are rare. The contemporary hobo is a different type entirely, with only a few similarities. For a short time here and there I lived a part of that growing folklore, seeing it at first hand.

Among the poems known by many were "Toledo Slim," "The Girl with the Blue Velvet Band," the well-known "Face on the Barroom Floor," "Down in Lehigh Valley," and "The Lure of the Tropics."

One remembered quatrain is typical:

I've juggled a tray in a New York café,
Hopped bells in a hotel in Chi.
I've carried a pack down the B & O track,
And hopped Red Ball freights on the fly.

Another, of the same vintage:

I've clerked in Kansas City,
Sold insurance in St. Paul,
Peddled books in Dallas, Texas,
And gone hungry in them all.

My intention had been to write, and consequently I had made no effort to acquire a trade. Naturally, living such a life one picks up certain knacks and skills but not enough to become expert at anything. All I had to offer was considerable physical strength and two hands, but for most jobs it was all that was required. I carried a hod, mixed concrete, shoveled sand or gravel, and dug ditches.

All the while I read. There was no plan, nor at the time could there be. One had to read what was available, and it had been so from the beginning.

Back in Jamestown there was a set of books called *The Rover Boys*, and I read however many there were. Several friends were reading them at the same time. We also read a series by Joseph A. Altsheler on the Civil and Revolutionary Wars.

Shortly before I entered the seventh grade I got my first job, the only one I was ever to get through influence or knowing somebody.

In this case it was a friend of my father's who was Vice-President of the Midland Continental Railroad (Peggy Lee's father worked for the same company), a small railroad that serviced a farming area. I had remarked to him that I was going to get my father to buy me a bicycle.

"Why don't you buy it yourself?" he asked.

Astonished, I told him I did not have any money. "Get a job and earn it," he suggested.

I was not quite twelve at the time and the idea had never occurred to me. He turned to a friend who was Secretary and Treasurer of the same railroad and asked, "What kind of jobs are there for youngsters?"

He suggested I work as a messenger boy. My father's friend invited me up to his office and dictated a letter to the Western Union recommending me for the job. The other man, who was also head of the local Chamber of Commerce, signed it as well, as did the County Engineer. Needless to say, I got the job.

At first, having no bicycle, I delivered the messages on foot, which called for a lot of walking. The job itself was a learning experience — in more ways than one. There were several typewriters around the place and I began typing on one of the spare machines. About that same time, one of the other messengers introduced me to pulp adventure magazines.

These were never found in my home, as my mother did not approve of them, and I doubt if my brothers or sisters ever looked at one until some of my own stories began to appear there, much later.

It was in the magazines that I first encountered Edgar Rice Burroughs and his stories "The Princess of Mars," "The Gods of Mars," and "The Warlords of Mars." (Much later I had a Colorado friend who named his two burros Edgar and Rice.)

Also at this time there was a magazine called *Science and Invention*, published by Hugo Gernsback, a name famous to all who know science fiction. Gernsback featured popular articles on various aspects of science, but he did more than that, for in the pages of *Science and Invention* he published the first modern stories of science fiction. Later, when the audience demanded it, he began to publish *Amazing Stories*, and the rest is history.

Reading a combination of science fact and fiction led me to Professor Percival Lowell's books on Mars, the planet he was studying from his Lowell Observatory near Flagstaff.

These were not, of course, the first nonfiction books I had read. The first was, I believe, a book called *The Genius of Solitude*, which I found in our Alfred Dickey Library in my hometown.

About that time I had decided I was not learning fast enough in school (I was twelve), and I was enormously curious about what was available. *The Genius of Solitude* devoted several chapters to various thinkers, as I recall, but the only one I remember now is Socrates.

Interested in everything, I also found in our library a very good book on the history of flying, going back to the beginnings of kite flying in China and Japan, making hot-air balloons out of gold beater's skin, and going on to the German who made more than seven hundred flights with gliders, but crashed and was killed on the eve of his first powered flight. There was also a good history of the submarine, and somewhere along the line I dipped into books on botany, geology, mineralogy, and more.

As those who read will understand, once my years at home were ended, I had little choice about what I read, for I had to accept what was available. When I found a library, I could choose, but many of the books I read during those knockabout years were what could be found in bunkhouses, ships' fo'c'sles (crew's quarters), and such places. Sometimes the discoveries were real gems; more often they were the casual reading of wandering men. Whatever the book, a reader reads.

There is no reason why anyone cannot get an education if he or she wants it badly enough and is persistent. Most cities have libraries, and often state libraries will mail books to a reader. Books are available on every conceivable subject and there are many very good "how to" books from which one can learn the basics of a trade.

My great good fortune was that from the beginning I was aware of books and their availability. But until I was eighteen or nineteen I simply read whatever I could find, with no preconceived notion of what I wanted to learn or become.

When I did settle down to acquire the rudiments of an education, the courses of study I chose were, I am sure, not those that would have been prescribed for me by any educator of whom I know, and it has been my good fortune to know a good many in these later years.

We probably had no more than two or three hundred books in my home when I was a child, but the library was available and we all used it constantly. I read *Lorna Doone* (a great favorite of my mother's), Kingsley's *Westward Ho!*, Jane Porter's *The Scottish Chiefs*, *Ivanhoe* by Sir Walter Scott, as well as *Ben Hur* and *The Fair God* by Lew Wallace.

When I was about thirteen I discovered Alexandre Dumas. There had been talk at home of *The Count of Monte Cristo* and *The Three Mus-*

keteers, and I had read both. It was a great day when I discovered on the shelves of the library a set of forty-eight volumes by Dumas, and I read them, every one.

One book has always led to another with me, as I suspect it does with many, and I went on to read Victor Hugo's *Les Misérables*, *The Hunchback of Notre Dame*, *The Man Who Laughs*, and *Toilers of the Sea*. The last-named was my favorite, for reasons I do not recall, unless it was because of man's titanic struggle with the sea. The idea of one man against the elements has always fascinated me, even before I had such experiences of my own.

Somewhere along the line I read a half-dozen novels by James Fenimore Cooper; and as with Balzac, enjoyed them.

About that time my education took another direction. My father and two older brothers had boxed, and I grew up knowing the rudiments. In the YMCA gym I worked out a few times with Labe Safro, who had been a crack welterweight and middleweight fighter during the days of Mike Gibbons, Mike O'Dowd, and Kid Graves. Labe was umpiring baseball in Jamestown and worked out every day. He was a phenomenal bag puncher and had punched bags in vaudeville, keeping ten bags going at once.

And then the Petrolle boys came to town.

Do what thy manhood bids thee do,
From none but self expect applause;
He noblest lives and noblest dies
Who makes and keeps his self-made laws.
— SIR RICHARD FRANCIS BURTON

3

Pete Petrolle was a lightweight fighter out of Schenectady, New York. His manager at the time was a former boxer who owned and operated a café in Jamestown. His name was Lee Shrankel; he was also, temporarily, manager of Pete's younger brother, Billy.

Pete was a good, tough, knowing fighter who had already become as good as he was ever to get. Billy, on the other hand, was just beginning a career that would take him to the top, where he would defeat several champions in over-weight matches (so the title was not at stake) but was never to win a championship himself. From featherweight to welterweight he fought all the good ones, and many of them were very, very good.

At the time there were at least twenty good fighters for every one there is now, and it was about the only way a young man could come off the streets and become somebody. Now, with basketball and football paying enormous sums, there are many other ways to reach the top, and even common labor pays more in a day than one received in a week in the 1920's.

Competition in the ring was very tough and a boy had to be good to get anywhere at all. Usually that meant a year or two fighting four- or six-round bouts before a fighter got a shot at anything longer. During those years he was learning, discovering how to cope with the different styles of fighting, and refining his own. Probably the last fighter who went through that mill was Sugar Ray Robinson, who was also one of the greatest.

How I met Pete Petrolle I do not recall, but evidently I heard he was looking for somebody to spar with. I was fourteen, but tall, with a good reach, and I knew enough about boxing to take care of myself. In the next few weeks I learned a lot more. I would guess I worked at least fifty rounds with Pete on various days before I met Billy, and then I worked with them both. They took it easy with me, but I enjoyed the workouts and was learning rapidly.

At the time a boxing magazine was published in St. Paul, Minnesota (one of the great fight towns in its day). It was printed on pink paper like the more famous *Police Gazette* and was called the *Boxing Blade*. Aside from articles on boxers and boxing, old and new, it also published the decisions in fights all over the world. These decisions usually covered two or three pages in relatively fine print, and I was an avid reader of this weekly, with a good memory for who had fought whom and the result. I also learned how certain fighters reacted to southpaws, fancy-dan boxers, and the like.

None of this interfered with my reading, which continued in every spare moment.

Our library was a gift to the town by Alfred

Dickey and was named for him. He was known to both my parents but had passed on, I believe, before my time of awareness. Certainly no gift ever presented to a community was more appreciated, and especially so by me. The foundation of my education was laid there, and I learned not only how to use a library but what unexpected riches may lie hidden away on dusty shelves. That library was the first of many in my life, and I spent hours there, dipping into book after book, completing many.

It is often said that one has but one life to live, but that is nonsense. For one who reads, there is no limit to the number of lives that may be lived, for fiction, biography, and history offer an inexhaustible number of lives in many parts of the world, in all periods of time.

So it was with me. I saved myself much hardship by learning from the experiences of others, learning what to expect and what to avoid. I have no doubt that my vicarious experience saved me from mistakes I might otherwise have made — not to say I did not make many along the way.

No doubt reading *Martin Eden* by Jack London, as well as other life stories of writers, prepared me for the rejections to come, and the difficulty I would have in getting published. Because of what I had read I knew there would be rejections, but I had no idea there would be so many.

Hunger I was to experience many times, but it was reassuring to know others had survived, although most written accounts of hunger are by those who never experienced it. Knut Hamsun is the only one I can think of offhand who wrote with any knowledge of the experience. In the movies one always sees a hungry man stuffing himself with food when first he gets a chance to eat. That's ridiculous, of course, for a truly hungry man eats very slowly, savoring every bite, and is almost overcome by having food at last. Moreover, hunger shrinks the stomach and one's capacity is slight. On the second and third day after hunger, of course, there is no satisfying him. At first, he cannot eat very much. He does, however, long for food that *tastes*, something either spicy or sweet. At least, such has been my experience and that of others whom I have observed.

On at least three occasions I have gone four days without eating anything, and that after long periods of eating very little.

When in my stories I write of hunger, thirst, and cold, these things I have experienced. Here and there I've taken some brutal beatings, the worst of them in fights I won. I lost fights, too, in the amateur rings. Outside the ring I never lost a fight but my first one.

Often, when people hear of my career and the many jobs at which I worked, they believe I did this for writing experience. That's nonsense. I worked at those many jobs because work was hard to get and one took what was available at the time. During the Depression years and immediately before, jobs were scarce and a man had to keep hustling to keep working. A job might last for an hour or two, or perhaps for several days, and often weeks went by with no work at all.

All loose things seem to drift down to the sea, and so did I. Perhaps it was the sea stories I had read, or even some inherited memory, if there are such things, but I drifted down to the waterfronts and wound up with a seaman's job I was glad to get. What I did not know was that no one wanted to ship aboard that old craft and they had a hard time getting a crew. If there was anything to read aboard that ship but a few battered magazines, I never found it. In any event there was no time. When I came off watch I fell into my bunk, happy to have even a few minutes' rest.

On my second trip to sea, out of Galveston, Texas, to Liverpool and Manchester, England, there were books. Not many, but books nonetheless. If I recall correctly I was shipped as a deck boy. Supposedly a deck boy is an apprentice officer, but actually he, or at least I, functioned as an ordinary seaman but without equal wages.

People who live away from the sea often assume a merchant marine sailor has joined some kind of a service similar to the Navy.

Nothing of the kind. He is simply a seagoing laborer who wears no uniform and works in any clothes he may have or can buy from the Slop Chest (a store aboard a ship where a seaman can buy such odds and ends of clothing or equipment as are necessary). Although on most ships he will stand a wheel watch, he will also spend much time chipping rust, touching up the chipped spots with red lead paint, and then painting over with the ship's colors, whatever they may be.

There is never any scarcity of work at sea. The First Mate and the Bo'sun see to that.

The title of the first book I read aboard the S.S. *Steadfast* has long been forgotten. It was, however, an attempt to prove that the plays of Shakespeare were actually written by Christopher Marlowe. Marlowe had been killed in what was called a tavern brawl in Deptford, England. More likely it was a planned assassination, for all involved had been engaged in undercover work.

Marlowe had written a number of successful plays in the same general style as that adopted by Shakespeare, including *Tamburlaine the Great* and *The Jew of Malta*. The story I read aboard the *Steadfast* maintained that instead of Marlowe's being killed, another man was buried in his place (this is also claimed to be the story of both Billy the Kid and Jesse James). Marlowe then hid out in an old abbey, writing the plays which were produced under the name of his actor friend William Shakespeare. I thought then and think now this was arrant nonsense.

Many people seem offended that Shakespeare, who never attended a university, could write so brilliantly, and ever since his fame began, there have been efforts to prove that a dozen other people wrote his plays, including Sir Francis Bacon, who never managed to find the time to complete the work so dear to him in philosophy.

Known in his time largely as an actor, Shakespeare wrote his plays for his company at the Globe, of which he was part owner. Many of his plays and some of his poetry had been published, but his plays were not collected until after his death. He was considered a journeyman writer of some importance in his time, though many did not rank him, for example, with Ben Jonson or Marlowe.

Shakespeare's plays were written for a popular audience of some four hundred years ago, an audience made up largely of artisans and their apprentices, a few shopkeepers, and whoever else could be drawn to buy a ticket. His sources were few and are well known, but he was very topical. His play *The Tempest* was based on an actual shipwreck in the Bermudas which was a big news story at the time.

A mistake constantly made by those who should know better is to judge people of the past by our standards rather than their own. The only way men or women can be judged is against the canvas of their own time.

Elizabethan England was not a time given to introspection. It was a time of action, of often swift, heedless action. One must remember that this was the time of Sir John Hawkins, of Sir Francis Drake, of Sir Martin Frobisher and Sir Walter Raleigh; it was a time when the British were sailing into the harbor of Cadiz and sinking ships under the guns of a fort.

Hamlet, for example, needs to be read in terms

of the time. He has usually been portrayed by those who did not understand him at all, or were trying to view him through Freudian eyes rather than those of his own time.

His problem was very real. His suspicions might be great, but what evidence did he have? The word of a ghost. Shakespeare, several times in the play, touches upon the various attitudes toward ghosts, but the prevailing opinion was that ghosts were manifestations of the Devil.

So what did Hamlet have? The word of the Devil suggesting he kill a king? To kill a king at any time was a serious matter, and especially so for a prince who would inherit the throne. Hamlet was not a weak character but a strong one. But he was also a reasonable man. He had to have more evidence, and he set about trying to get it.

Our working days aboard ship were divided into two four-hour watches, separated by eight-hour interludes. A seaman on the *Steadfast*, as on many other ships, spent two hours each day and two hours each night at the wheel. At night he also spent two hours on lookout in the bow. By day the two hours were devoted to work around the deck. Deck boys or ordinary seamen, however, spent all their time working, keeping things shipshape under direction of the Bo'sun. (The word is properly *boatswain*, but I never heard it spoken in that way.) Often when chipping rust or touching up paint, I thought about what I had been reading, and as our ship was heading for England, recalling the book on Marlowe and Shakespeare was especially interesting.

On that voyage I also read Jack London's *The Sea Wolf*, H. Rider Haggard's *The Ivory Child*, and *The White Company* by Arthur Conan Doyle. The latter book, by the creator of Sherlock Holmes, was the story of a company of mercenaries, an exciting, romantic story.

The voyage over was rough and I had my first bout with seasickness off Cape Hatteras, my first and my worst. It lasted for three days. On my previous voyage I had come through a West Indies hurricane and had the mistaken idea I was immune. Cape Hatteras proved me wrong, as it has many another seafaring man. Our return trip was by way of the Azores and a relatively calm, easy voyage with sun-filled days, beautiful starlit nights, and only the very slightest roll to the ship; not at all like those days on the way over when the Bo'sun would look into the fo'c'sle and yell, "All out! Sea boots and oilskins!" Which meant it was raining, we were shipping seas (taking on water), or both.

The *Steadfast* was a flush-decker of, if I recall correctly, 4,800 tons.*

We had only a couple of weeks in England and, as was usually the case, never got far from the waterfront. We docked in Liverpool, where the main hangout was the American Bar on Lime Street, or the London Wine House not far away.

*A flush-decker is a ship not having a superstructure above the freeboard deck.

43

I was sixteen, passing as twenty-two, but not interested in drinking. I had ideas that I might make boxing a career, and had worked hard to get myself and keep myself in shape.

One of my particular friends aboard ship was an able-bodied seaman (called an A.B.) named Harry Warren, referred to usually as Shorty.

He was an Australian, an excellent seaman except that, like Lord Nelson, he was seasick on every trip. Why he continued to follow the sea under the circumstances I have no idea, but he did. In Manchester — actually in Salford — Shorty introduced me to a strong-arm man named Reggie, who worked the waterfronts. Reggie taught me several tricks of waterfront fighting that were often useful. One was the so-called Liverpool Kiss, where you catch a man behind his neck and jerk his face down to meet your upcoming skull. Done properly it can obliterate, for the time being, a man's features and make him less than anxious to pursue the argument. Education, you see, has many aspects.

Shorty had been around and he had friends. Never a drinker, he knew his way about the seaports of the world and had made friends in them all. Aboard ship he had a mandolin he had made himself and which he played, singing many of the old sea chanteys as well as British, Irish, and Scottish folk songs.

Another particular friend aboard ship was Pete Boering, a big Dutchman from Amsterdam, and perhaps the finest merchant seaman I was ever to meet. He was twenty-eight at the time I knew him and had spent eighteen years at sea, starting as cabin boy on his father's own ship.

When fifteen he had been washed overboard during a typhoon. They threw him a life ring, which he got, but they were unable to pick him up. Three days later he was found by an Australia-bound vessel and taken there. In the years that followed he had never been home.

It was the old story, dramatized by Eugene O'Neill (himself a merchant seaman for a time) in *The Long Voyage Home*. A sailor saves his money, planning to return home to see his family but not wishing to go empty-handed. Once ashore, everybody wishes him well and somebody suggests a farewell drink. Hours later the seaman is back aboard a ship, broke again.

Pete was planning to go home when I met him, and he was planning to go home when I last saw him, on the docks in Houston.

With a few dollars saved, I grabbed an armful of boxcars and headed west, again on the Southern Pacific. Before boarding the freight train I stopped at a newsstand and bought a double handful of Little Blue Books.

I do not now remember all the titles, but I know I had Oscar Wilde's "The Ballad of Reading Gaol," Charles Finger's *Great Escapes*, and a collection of Emerson's essays.

4

The trip west was a rough one. For the first time when riding freights I had enough, although barely enough, for occasional meals. It was never advisable to allow those with whom you traveled to know you had money, however little. Moreover, I was anxious not to arrive home without some money. This was my first venture into the world alone and I wished to return with enough to hold me until I could find a job.

As always, I found myself traveling with three others, and several times we were put off the train and had to wait to catch a later one. At such times we gathered about a fire in the hobo "jungle" and swapped stories. Mostly, I listened.

One of the men, a machinist, was promised a job in El Paso, if he could get there. He had left his wife and two children in Shreveport to wait until he could send for them. What money he had, he'd left with them, taking only six dollars for the trip. Mentally, I crossed my fingers for him, for I had already learned that promises are often lightly made with no expectation that a man would travel so far for a job.

Another of the men was a black boxer, a welterweight who looked good. In those days, boxing in California was limited to four rounds per fight, and he had been told he would do well out there, with his style. We sat in the door of an empty boxcar and talked of fights and fighters, and of many of the good black fighters, including Tiger Flowers, a middleweight out of Georgia who was one of the best in the game, as long as he could stay away from Jack Delaney, a light heavyweight who had his number and knocked him out twice.

In El Paso our machinist friend went his way while I bought a few Little Blue Books, including "The Rime of the Ancient Mariner" and some shorter pieces by Coleridge. The black fighter got off there, too, after seeing a poster advertising a fight. He was hoping they might need another boxer in the event that someone failed to appear, as was sometimes the case.

Inadvertently I found myself in the company of a young steelworker who had never been away from home before and never out of a job. He had only himself to worry about, but was overwhelmed with self-pity. When I told him of the machinist he was not impressed. The only tragedy he could grasp was his own, and he seemed to feel the world out there should have been waiting for him with open arms.

A tough railroad detective put us off the train in the desert on a lonely siding at night. Hustling around, and with no help from the young man, I found some fragments of wood and a few mesquite branches and started a fire. Several times in the bitterly cold night I awakened to add fuel

48

to keep our fire going. My traveling companion never stirred, and it was so cold I could not get back to sleep.

The same thing happened on the third night, but on the morning following, a train was side-tracked to allow a passenger train to pass and we scrambled aboard, finding an empty car where we could keep out of sight. For the rest of the day he complained and I read Coleridge. In Deming, New Mexico, we were again put off the train and found the town filled with drifters like ourselves who had been put off trains and were unable to get out.

Every possible job had been done long ago and there was no chance for work. What money I had I kept out of sight. I watched for a chance to leave town, and hoped to leave my traveling companion behind, but he clung to me like lint to a blue serge suit, and when I finally got out west of town and snagged a westbound freight, he was right with me.

Each night in Deming we slept out, and each night I built the fire and kept it going, and each night, once awakened by the cold, I found it virtually impossible to get back to sleep. My traveling companion never so much as budged. Somebody, he was sure, would take care of him. He was his mother's boy and somebody always had.

The end came at Stein's Pass, New Mexico. We were put off the train there and ducked into the small station, where there was a potbellied stove, glowing and red, and we were *cold*. The station agent and telegrapher let us huddle close to the fire until the time came for him to close up.

"I'd like to let you stay, boys, but I've got to lock up."

Reluctantly, we went out into the cold wind and found our way into a hollow near the tracks. There, with little help, I gathered some coal from along the track, some scraps of wood, and built a fire.

"Look," I told him. "Night after night I've kept the fire going and you've slept. Several times you told me you'd wake up and you haven't. Now I'm dead tired. I'm ready to drop. Tonight you've got to wake up."

He promised he would. I added coal to the fire and we lay as close to it as we could without burning.

At four o'clock in the morning I awakened, my teeth chattering. The fire was out, and the ashes were cold. Neither of us had another match, but he slept peacefully, blissfully. For a moment I thought of kicking him awake and knocking him down when he started to get up, but then I was afraid he would follow me when I went away. So I left him sleeping peacefully and walked away through what there was of the silent town, and headed down the road toward Tucson, somewhere far off to the west.

I never saw him again, and never wished to. It was many years before I visited Stein's Pass again, and on that occasion it was just after my wife and I had left the film set of *Heller in Pink*

Tights, a movie made from one of my stories,* with Anthony Quinn, Sophia Loren, and Steve Forrest.

Wishing to see again the area I had written about in *Shalako*, Kathy and I drove east into New Mexico, and stopped briefly at Stein's Pass. The street was empty, the buildings falling down, and nobody in sight. Almost thirty years had passed, so I did not expect to see my former traveling companion. No doubt, wherever he is, somebody is building fires for him, or maybe he took the time to grow up and become a man.

When I walked away from Stein's Pass, I had never considered writing a western story. At home I had been brought up on stories of Indians and Indian fighting but writing about them had not entered my mind. I did plan to write, to tell stories, but the nature of those stories was something that remained to be seen.

However, I was used to listening to older people talk, and enjoyed their stories. Moreover, I had an insatiable curiosity about places and people, so I was never content to just pass through a town. I wanted to know about it, how it came to be where it was, and who was responsible. I wanted to know about the country, and had read just enough in geology and botany to know something of land formations and plants.

Education, as I have said, takes many forms and

Heller With a Gun

there are many ways to knowledge and awareness. From the very beginning of my knocking about, I tried to learn about the country I was seeing, and soon discovered that in any hamburger stand or restaurant, in any barbershop or filling station, there is somebody who knows the area, or can direct you to somebody who does.

Usually a question was all that was needed. If the one questioned did not know, someone was sure to overhear and respond.

Before I was ever to read of them in books or diaries, I heard stories of John Wesley Hardin, John Selman, Jim Gillette, and Jeff Milton. The stories were told in the places where they happened, although often details or dates were mistaken, to be corrected later.

Too often, though, in the places where travelers or tourists stopped, I would hear men boast only of the miles covered that day, rarely of what they had seen. I must say that is less true today, but for many years people were enthralled with distance covered, not what country they had passed through or what they had seen.

Every road in the United States, or any other country, has its places of interest. There was an evening in Colorado when we walked into a restaurant just as a man we had seen that morning was paying his check.

"What happened to you?" he asked. "Saw you this morning when we started. Just get in?"

"We stopped to see the old stage station," I told him.

He looked blank, then curious. "What stage station?"

"You drove right by it. Interesting old place. Jack Slade, the gunfighter, used to hang out there."

They are out there by the thousands, wonderful stories. Many have never gotten into the histories, although occasionally told by local newspapers or in privately printed booklets. Stories of wagon-train massacres, buried treasures, gun battles, cattle roundups, border bandit raids — no matter where you go, east, west, north, and south, there are stories. People are forever asking me where I get my ideas, but one has only to listen, to look, and to live with awareness. As I have said in several of my stories, all men look, but so few can see. It is all there, waiting for any passerby.

There was an old man in Kingman, Arizona, who would tell stories to anybody who would listen. People around town scoffed. "Aw, he's full of hot air. Don't pay any attention." Or, "He's an old liar."

Well, I listened. True or not, they were good stories, and years later nearly every one checked out. Here was a rich repository of history and legend, and nobody was listening.

Stein's Pass was right in the middle of what had been Apache country, and not far from there was Doubtful Canyon, of which I would write. Getting kicked off that freight train gave me a chance to see some of that country for the first time.

It had been bitterly cold during the night but as day broke I found myself walking down a gravel road in lonely desert and mountain country with lots of distance everywhere and nothing that might be a roadside filling station or a ranch. If I did not get a ride I was going to be in serious trouble for water. My only hope was to keep going and hope this untraveled road merged with a highway somewhere ahead.

When I had walked at least five miles I heard a car coming up behind me, and I stopped, looking hopeful.

The driver was a big old man, neatly dressed and wearing a white hat, a white mustache, and perhaps the sharpest eyes I had seen in years. He asked if I wanted a lift, which we both knew was an idle question.

"I'm heading for Phoenix," I said, hoping he might be going there himself.

"Thought you might be from one of the ranches. How'd you get out here?"

So I explained about being put off the freight train, and added that I had a chance of a job in Phoenix. Then I commented, "I hate to leave here without seeing Doubtful Canyon."

He almost stopped the car. "What do you know about Doubtful Canyon?"

So I told him about working with an old man in the Panhandle of Texas who had been raised by Apaches, a white boy who had ridden with Geronimo and Cochise as well as Nana. He had told me about his first war party, which was an attack on a stage in Doubtful Canyon.

He questioned me about where and how I had

known the man and what he had told me. "Boy," he said, "you had a piece of history right there with you. That was a famous fight."

He looked at me again. "You had breakfast, son?"

"No, sir. I started out of Stein's Pass before daylight."

"We'll eat breakfast," he said. "I want to hear more about this Indian."

He was not an Indian, I told him, except by training and feeling. He was a white man who had been captured as a boy. He believed his family was Swedish but he wasn't even sure about his name anymore.

We stopped at Bowie, eating breakfast at a roadside restaurant. People there knew the man who was driving me. The waitress looked at me and asked him: "You got you a prisoner?"

"He's a friend."

"Are you the Law?" I asked him.

"In a way. Have you anything against the Law?"

"My father was an officer up in North Dakota," I said. "He was a veterinarian but was a deputy sheriff too. And the man who taught me how to use a six-shooter was an officer. He was one of the old-time gunfighters."

"Who might that be?" He was skeptical.

"Bill Tilghman," I said. "He was a friend of my brother's in Oklahoma City."

"Heard of him. Heard he was a good man."

We talked our breakfast away and then drove on. He was going as far as Tucson, he told me, and would carry me that far.

We discovered we had both read Porter's *Scottish Chiefs* and Scott's *Marmion*. He knew a lot about gunfighters and talked of John Wesley Hardin. "I knew him," he added, "and the man who killed him."

Now I was skeptical, and he explained. "I was Chief of Police in El Paso, and before that I was a Texas Ranger."

Any conversation reproduced after years is a matter of guesswork, but that was the gist of it.

I told him of baling hay in the Pecos Valley and of meeting Tom Pickett, who was spending a few weeks there, and of meeting George Coe and Deluvina Maxwell, all of whom had known Billy the Kid.

The old-timers I'd met were men he had either known or knew of. He had strong opinions, with some of which I did not agree, but I was not there to argue but to learn. Young as I was, I had learned that gunfighters themselves had definite opinions about others with such reputations. Those whom they had known were generally respected; those they had not known were apt to be disparaged.

He dropped me off on a corner in Tucson.

"If you're up this way again, son, look me up. I enjoyed the talk. You just ask for Jeff Milton. Folks will know me."

The dogs bark, but the caravan passes on.
— ORIENTAL PROVERB

5

This is the tale as it was told to me by the smoke of a cow-chip fire, at night on the Panhandle plains of West Texas. I was sixteen, passing as twenty-two, and the old man was pushing eighty but did not remember his actual age. Nor did he know his whiteman's name.

We had been hired by a wolfer and trapper who had made a deal to skin cattle killed by drought on a big ranch. Around every windmill dead cattle could be found, numbering from fifteen to thirty-five, and saving their hides was a job only for someone with a strong stomach.

The wolfer was named Peterson, and when the old man heard the name he said he thought it was his own. Anyway, the name was familiar.

His father, he said, was a brute, a big, raw-boned man who worked his son like a slave and treated him worse. Once his mother died, the boy was taken from school, where he had spent just one year, and put to work. When the Apaches raided their homestead, his father fought like a tiger, but was killed.

When a warrior was about to kill the boy, another Apache stopped him. "I take," he said. "You fight like him, you my son."

Peterson, as he now called himself, had never looked back. From that time on he was an Apache and wished to be nothing else. His life as a white boy had been hard and cruel; among the Indians he was better treated and he worked hard to be one of them. He believed he was almost seven when taken by the Apache, and five years later he rode on his first war party.

He was not allowed to fight. He went with others of about his age to care for horses, to gather wood for fires, to cook meat for the braves, and to learn by watching and listening.

They were going after a stage said to be coming from the east, and they would attack near Stein's Peak, which marked the entrance to what white men called Doubtful Canyon.

The canyon was eight to ten miles long, depending on who was measuring, and its name resulted from the fact that, during Apache days, if you went in, it was doubtful you'd get out.

On this day, Apache signals had made them aware the stage was coming soon after it left Cooke's Spring near Deming, New Mexico. Cochise and even the chief Mangas Colorado, had gathered their warriors to attack near East Garrison Station at the entrance to Doubtful Canyon.

It was a hot, still day, his first war party. Peterson remembered it well. Crouched among the rocks atop a canyon wall, he watched the stage approaching, his heart pounding. No warriors were in sight until the stage entered the canyon. Then, like magic, the canyon walls were lined with them. The only location that offered a chance for defense was a rocky knoll at one side of the trail.

Watching from the rocks, the boy saw a sudden splash of crimson across a horse's shoulder and saw the animal stumble, then go down, piling up in a mass of struggling horses and a tangle of harness. The pursuing stage overran the horses and overturned, the men spilling out, rifles in hand.

At once they began to shoot, while some struggled to haul boxes from the stage. From high on the cliffside he could see it all, bright in the sunlight.

There were seven men. He counted them. They had rifles and pistols, and the boxes must contain ammunition. They fell into position and began shooting. The Apaches went to cover, leaving several of their number dead upon the rocks.

The watching boy moved into the shade of a rock. There was no shade for the fighting men on the knoll, and the sun was blistering. They ranged themselves around the rocks to cover all approaches. It was not a good position, for many parts of the knoll were exposed, but the stage itself helped. It was no protection against bullets but it did protect against the iron-tipped arrows.

One of the white men was down. He must be dead, as there was no effort to pull him closer, although another man did take his rifle and ammunition belt.

The Apaches did not know it then, and the Peterson boy, if that was his name, only learned it long after, but the Free Thompson Party, the men in that stagecoach, had thousands of rounds of ammunition. What they did not have was food. Even more important, they had no water, and there was no water hole nearer than Stein's Peak, several miles away.

From where the boy watched, he could see it all, but the distance was too great for a rifle to fire with accuracy.

The rocks were hot to his touch — blistering, in fact. It must be pure Hell down in that oven of a canyon where no wind blew and no air stirred. All day the fighting went on, and the canyon walls echoed with gunfire. When night fell, the guns were silent, but the Apaches — who did not like to fight at night because, they were reported to believe, if one was killed in the dark, his spirit must forever wander in darkness — still gathered close around. Peterson knew there was no chance for the white men to escape, and they knew it as well.

Down there among the scattered rocks and the wreck of the stagecoach, men would be smoking, chewing tobacco, watching, and resting.

They had no hope of escape. No cavalry would be coming to their rescue, for the pony soldiers had gone east to fight in the War Between the States. They would be bandaging wounds down there, holding pebbles in their mouths to alleviate thirst, and piling rocks to make their position more secure.

Beside the smoky cow-chip fire, the old man told the story of that desperate fight so long ago, the first one he had witnessed. He told of the coming of light which showed how well the white men had worked during the night, gathering rocks to fill spaces between boulders, making their position more secure. The bloating bodies of the dead horses were a protection, too, but there were only five men moving about now, and hundreds of Indians.

The boy did not know how many Apaches there were, for both Cochise and Mangas Colorado had brought warriors, while his group had come from Nana's band.

There was only sporadic fighting now, for the Apaches had suffered. Bodies lay stretched on the sand and hanging over rocks to indicate the accuracy of the white-eyes' shooting. A half hour might go by without a shot, and then some ill-advised Indian would show himself and die for his carelessness.

Searching fire from Apache rifles sought hidden targets, chancing shots into the stagecoach in hopes some man might be using it for shelter, but the thin walls and floor of the stage were no protection against .44 caliber bullets, which could penetrate several inches of pine.

Occasionally a group of Apaches would attempt an attack and there would be a burst of firing.

The boys watching from the ridge could see little movement now. Were more men dead? Or were they guarding their strength? Boards had been pulled from the splintered stage in an effort to make some sort of a shield from the sun. Again the day passed, and again night came with no shooting, and only a waiting time until the morrow.

There is no way I can tell that story as it was told to me beside the smoky fire on the plains of the Panhandle, told to me by the old man who remembered it so well, a white man who had become completely an Apache, and was in his heart and mind an Apache still.

The third day dawned, a third day of terrible thirst and gnawing hunger, a third day of desperation. How many were left? The boys watching from the crest could not tell, but whenever an Apache moved, a rifle spoke from the rocky knoll.

At last, midway in the third afternoon, the shooting ended, and after a long time Apaches began to expose themselves. When there was no more firing they went down, one after another, until hundreds of them were gathered.

The ammunition was all gone. One of the last men had broken the extra rifles so they would not be available for use by the Apaches.

Apaches carried their dead away and rarely admitted their losses, but the reports were that between 130 and 150 Apaches died in that three-day fight. All seven of the defenders died, the last one, or perhaps two, dying by his own hand with his last bullet, rather than suffer the torture that awaited him if taken alive.

Long after, in Chihuahua, Cochise was said to have told of the battle and declared they were the bravest men he ever knew.

If that was true, I do not know. I only know the story that was told to me that night by the dim light from a smoky fire.

It was the first of many stories told over fires, tales of swift attacks and long pursuits by the pony soldiers and the tactics the Indians used. Years later, some of it was to appear in *Hondo*, some in *Shalako* and in *The Lonely Men*. But at the time I had no idea of ever writing about what I was experiencing then, or of what I was hearing.

Yet there was no better time to learn about what the West had actually been. Many of those who lived it were still alive, and as the years of their future grew fewer, they were more willing to talk of what had been. Old feuds were largely forgotten, and time had given the past an aura.

The old cowboy might appear to be as dry as dust, he might scoff at some of the stories, but he was a figure of romance in his own mind (although he would never have admitted it) or he would not have become a cowboy in the first place. As the years slipped away, he began to want to tell his stories, and I was often there, a willing listener, knowing enough to sift the truth from the romance.

In every town there was at least one former outlaw or gunfighter, an old Indian scout or a wagon master, and each with many stories ready to tell.

One story engendered another, and sitting on a bench in front of a store I'd tell of something I knew or had heard and would often get a story in return, sometimes a correction. The men and women who lived the pioneer life did not suddenly disappear; they drifted down the years, a rugged, proud people who had met adversity and survived. Once, many years later, I was asked in a television interview what was the one quality that distinguished them, and I did not come up with the answer I wanted. Later, when I was in the hotel alone, it came to me.

Dignity.

They all had dignity, a certain serenity and pride that was theirs completely. They might be poor, they might be eking out at the last a precarious living, but they had dignity.

They knew where they had been and what they had seen and done, and were content. Something was theirs, something within themselves that neither time passing nor man nor hard times could take from them.

I have worked beside them, eaten at their tables, sat beside them in sunlight and moonlight and firelight. I never knew one of the old breed who did not have it.

It was hard work skinning those dead cattle, brutal, messy work, and I did not like it, but a job was a job, and I needed a road stake to go on to wherever it was I was going. Often at night, after the old man had turned in, I stirred the fire, adding hoarded mesquite roots, and read by the firelight.

The book was *Gil Blas*, a copy I had found abandoned in the laundry room of a tourist court in

Plainview, Texas. Whether it was left by intent or accident, I could not know, but it was my good fortune. I'd known of the book for years but had never happened upon it before, so I read it, not once but twice, on the plains of West Texas.

What someone else in my position might have done I am not sure. Very likely, when they paid off such a job as I had, they might have gone on a three-day drunk. What I did was get a room in a small hotel and take three showers a day, finding my way, in between times, to the library, where I began reading John Motley's *The Rise of the Dutch Republic*, and when I finished that, I went west.

Which brings me back to Tucson, where this digression began. All the above took place months before I was put off the freight train at Stein's Pass, but is an example of the stories that lurk everywhere, awaiting the lucky finder. The story of Doubtful Canyon and the fight is well known in the area and by many historians of the Apache wars, but I heard it from a spectator. Thirty years later I could have thought of a thousand questions to ask. Then, I merely listened and remembered, and that was the story I told Jeff Milton in the restaurant in Bowie.

Tired of hitching rides, and expecting no luck on the busy highway to Phoenix, I bought a ticket on a bus. A week later I was digging holes to plant a citrus grove near Phoenix. (Unhappily, a few years later, the trees were all removed to make way for a housing development in what is now one of the plushier areas of the city.) That job ended all too quickly, and with no local prospects, I started north.

On the Black Canyon Road my ride stopped to fix a tire. Another car stopped near us and the driver came over. He needed a man to be caretaker at a mine. He studied me. "Could I stand to be alone?" I could.

"The last man who said that lasted almost two weeks. This is really *alone*," he warned.

My nearest neighbor lived in a mine tunnel about a mile away, was an Indian, and crazy. Anybody who came close he suspected of trying to steal his mine. The old Indian carried a pistol and was a dead shot.

"Stay away from him. He'll kill you as soon as look at you," the man added.

When asked, he volunteered that there was plenty of reading material. I was to live on the place, see that no trespassers carried away any tools, feed the dogs and chickens, and do the assessment work.

I took the job.

6

The mine lay in a basin at the end of thirty-odd miles of winding one-lane dirt road. A very rocky road, I might add, most of it built by use. There was a mine shaft down about one hundred and seventy feet, a half mile of drifts* (which I never saw, as the mine was filled with water up to about forty feet from the surface), and there was a hoisting-engine and a compressor, both in excellent shape.

A bit away from the mine there was a boarding house, a concrete bunkhouse with ten rooms that slept two men each. There were two dogs and about sixty white Leghorn chickens.

All around were rocky bluffs and hills scattered with sparse semi-desert growth. A dry wash came out of the hills and swung around the mine area, dropping off into a narrow, rocky gulch about a half mile in length.

My new boss left me off, turned around, and drove away. I was alone.

From what I gathered in the drive out to the mine, there had been several others who attempted the caretaking job, the last being a schoolteacher who had come with two projects: to do a lot of

*Horizontal passageways in underground mining.

serious study and to become a fine rifle and pistol shot. He had moved out there with a thousand rounds of ammo, two dozen excellent books, several blank notebooks, a number of sharp pencils, and a lot of ambition. What kind of teacher he was I never learned, nor who he was. To be alone was what he wanted.

The difficulty was that few people know what it means to be absolutely alone. Even fewer know what silence is. Our lives are filled with the coming and going of people and vehicles, so much so that our senses scarcely notice the sounds. They have become a background to all our living, all our thinking, absorbed subconsciously.

Suddenly, here, the man was *alone*. There was no sound. Occasionally, during the day, a hen might cackle, a loosened pebble might rattle down the rocks. Otherwise, nothing.

The mine was at the end of a road down which nobody drove. Whoever the young man was, he had not bargained for this. No doubt he had told himself how wonderful it would be simply to study without fear of interruption, to be alone in the hills. No doubt it sounded poetic as well.

It was not Walden Pond. There was no water here except what came from a well. There were no forests. There wasn't a tree within miles. The only birds he saw were magpies who teased the dogs, and the blue quail running through the low brush. Occasionally there was a hawk or golden eagle at which the dogs barked to keep them from the chickens.

His investment must have been at least $300 in books, ammunition, and guns. Perhaps it was more, though prices were reasonable then. Except for that investment, he might have left sooner, but I suspect that by the third day the silence was beginning to bother him. At first he would have brushed it off, telling himself he would get used to it. By the fifth day he would not have been as sure.

Some of what had gone on I found in rolled-up wads of note paper where he had begun to write, but he rarely got past the middle of the page before discarding it.

Then the pages had only a line or two — I gathered he was trying to do something on Shakespeare — and after that, often blank pages were discarded.

My first days at the mine were busy ones. I cleaned out the room in which I planned to sleep, made up the cot, and hung out the few clothes I had. Then I checked out the boarding house to see what food was available. It was mostly canned goods, which pleased me, as I was no kind of a cook and hoped to do as little as possible. Then I scouted the place where I was to do the assessment work.

It was a tunnel only a few feet deep, striking into the mountain toward what they hoped was a vein. I doubted there was anything there, but who was I to question? There was a pick and shovel hard by — and a short-handled pick, at that.

My predecessor's books were boxed but not

sealed up, and I went through them.

A complete volume of Shakespeare's plays, Robert Burton's *The Anatomy of Melancholy*, the short stories of O. Henry (I've forgotten how complete an edition, but *The Four Million* was there and, I believe, the story of the Cisco Kid — "The Caballero's Way," from *Heart of the West*). There was also a book of collected poetry by many writers (but the title forgotten), *The Autobiography of Joseph Jefferson*, a volume on the theater in Elizabethan England, and *Don Quixote*.

There were also translations of both the *Iliad* and the *Odyssey*, which I had dipped into several times but never read. Aside from the Shakespeare, on which the man obviously planned a paper, and O. Henry, which I decided was a personal preference, he seemed to have gathered such books as he had always wished to read but had not found time for.

According to the man who hired me, the teacher lasted nearly two weeks and then just dropped everything and walked away, calling him from the first telephone he found to say he was through. Having said that, the young man hung up, and that was the end of it.

My boss suspected, however, there had been more to it than loneliness. He suspected the old Indian up on the mountain had spooked him.

Certainly, the old man did prowl about, often at night, but I didn't mind and the dogs no longer barked at him. He came and went like a ghost, active as a goat, although he was said to be past ninety years. Certainly his features looked old enough to have worn out two or three bodies.

Later, I was to meet him, and he was another part of my education, for he taught me much of food plants and Indian remedies — the first Indian I knew but for one I met at Puerto de Luna on my trail to Fort Sumner.

At this point I simply read what was available, with an insatiable appetite. I might add that, aside from the books (of which I've listed scarcely half) left by the teacher, there were other books left by miners or owned by the proprietor. Among these were several volumes by Clarence E. Mulford, who wrote the Hopalong Cassidy series; a couple of novels by Zane Grey; B. M. Bower's *Chip of the Flying U*; and novels by James Oliver Curwood and Harold Bell Wright. There was also *The Spoilers* by Rex Beach. Some of these were on a dusty shelf in the boarding house. Others I found in various rooms of the empty bunkhouse.

The owner had subscribed to *The Saturday Evening Post* and several years' worth of them were stacked on the floor in the boarding house.

I had been alone before, but made companions of the dogs and often walked the hills with one or the other. I had been warned not to let them loose together, for they would pull down and kill cattle on the range.

The assessment work was my first problem. I went to work on some rotten quartz, wheeling it to the dump nearby. Often I would take a break, drink coffee, and read. Then, as many times since,

73

I did not read from one book alone but started several, anxious to get the flavor of each one and reluctant to wait until one was finished before dipping into another.

Every book I read opened vistas before me of the things I did not know, of the books I had not read. I was not like Ivan, in *The Brothers Karamazov*, who wanted not millions but an answer to his questions. I did not even know the questions.

Questions must be formulated from knowledge and I knew too little for that. I was a young man in a hurry, wanting to know all that had been thought, pondered, speculated upon.

The world was out there, a big, wonderful, and exciting place of which I knew too little. In my reading I was constantly coming upon the names of scholars, historians, or political leaders of whom I knew nothing at all, though often enough there were names that I remembered from dinner-table talk at home. Reading *Don Quixote* was marvelous stuff, but I needed to know more about Cervantes himself and the world in which he lived.

The loneliness at the mine never affected me, for I had many companions: Hopalong Cassidy, Hamlet, Sancho Panza, and Ulysses were with me. I worked at the assessment job, sat on the muck-pile and read for a half hour or so, and then went back to the pick and shovel. In between times I walked on the hills with one or the other of the dogs.

There were two sheep left behind as lambs by

some passing sheepherder's flock and now grown to full size. The black-faced ram was young, full of mischief, and had to be watched. For fear of wolves or coyotes they never fed far from the mine, but when I walked out they often went with me, feeling secure in my presence. The first time they did this I was pleased, enjoying their company, and making friends, I thought, with the ram. Yet when I began to return on the first walk we took together, I heard a scramble of feet behind me and started to turn. Too late.

The ram butted me very solidly in the rear and knocked me sprawling on the gravel. I got up swearing and he trotted off to one side and eyed me complacently. Mission accomplished.

Every time the sheep followed me out, he attempted a repeat of what to him was vastly amusing, but he never again succeeded in catching me unawares, until almost my last day. Starting back, I suddenly saw that someone was at the mine. I forgot the ram and started to hurry, but too late I remembered — and he got me again. I skinned both knees on the rocky hillside.

There were wolves about, for at night I often heard them howling, although I do not believe there were more than four or five. Once, I actually saw one, trotting along the mountainside near an old corral. He was alone, and intent on some business of his own.

The lone visitor that day was the Indian from up on the mountain, the second time we had met.

The first time was when I was hiking down that

rocky gorge below the mine and thinking of nothing I can remember, when suddenly some sound or movement behind me turned me around.

The old Indian I had been warned about was behind me, wearing a sagging vest and a battered, narrow-brimmed hat, his legs bound in wrap-around leggings made from canvas. On his hip was the pistol of which I had been told. I stood aside and waited for him to overtake me, a bit jumpy inside. Yet I, too, was armed.

When I spoke he asked me if I had seen an old gray burro. I had, often, but not that day.

"If you see her," he said, "don't ride her. She's very old and not very strong. I know how boys are," he added, "but she's not up to it."

He had but one eye, the other merely an empty socket. We walked on, and a couple of times he stopped to gather weeds from alongside the trail. When asked, he told me they were a plant he used for medicine, and as I seemed curious, he explained about various plants as we walked along. Some were for food, some medicine, and some were used for dyes.

It was the first of a half-dozen such conversations we had, and each time I learned a little bit. Carefully, I avoided any question about where he lived or his mine. He obviously knew what I was doing and asked no questions either. I gathered that he did not like my boss.

We spotted a flock of Mexican blue quail moving through the brush and he drew and fired, clipping the head from one very neatly indeed. A few minutes later he repeated it, picking up the quail — obviously his dinner.

Once he came down to ask for eggs, which I gave him, adding some onions and potatoes. I never learned what kind of Indian he was, although for some reason I think that he was a Papago. It was not Papago country, however, so I could be wrong.

He was said to be over ninety years old and I could believe it, yet he was not a man one questioned, and I had been warned to show no interest. I am sure, looking back, that I missed a rare opportunity, for he seemed willing enough to talk when he opened the conversation.

The last three weeks I was there I saw him not at all.

And I never saw him again.

My assessment work was finished, and so were most of the books and ammunition. I had explored the country nearby and was beginning to feel the urge to move on. True, several of the books I had read while there could be read again with profit, but I was not prepared for that. There were too many books I had not read at all, and too many miles I had not covered.

Several times, just for luck, I had panned out some of the rotten quartz that I crushed with a double-jack (sledgehammer), but found no color.

In a small stream a few miles away I had better luck. In occasional attempts I panned out nearly $300 in gold, enough to buy some clothing and head on to the westward.

I wanted to write, and had made attempts while at the mine, finishing nothing, but learning a little. My first attempt at creative writing had come when I was twelve. I'd been visiting an uncle in Minnesota, and one day I climbed a tree, sat on a big branch looking out over the lake at his back door, and started a poem.

All I knew about poetry was that I enjoyed it, and the poem went on and on. I could always write more but could find no ending. Somewhere around I still have it, a melancholy piece of no value.

Most of what I attempted at the mine were short stories, but unhappily I did not even know what a story was, although I believed I did. They were mostly pieces of narration without drama or anything else to recommend them. I was, however, trying. And I was putting words together, learning to shape my thoughts into something worth reading. There was much to learn, and I had no idea how rocky the road could be. Jack London's *Martin Eden* gave me some idea of what might lie ahead. It was to be a rough and lonely road, but it was the only road for me.

With what I had saved I bought new clothes, for those I'd taken to the mine had been worn out, and I headed for the sea again.

It was in my mind, vaguely, that I might "do" a Joseph Conrad. I might return to the sea, get my Third Mate's ticket, and begin writing at sea as he had. It was an idea that stayed with me for several years but never came to fruition.

The bus I was riding stopped in Ash Fork so

we could eat. We all rushed for the lunch counter to get our orders in while we could. We ate quickly and rushed back to the bus. I reached up for my suitcase. . . .

It was gone.

Much is not dared because it seems hard; much seems hard only because it is not dared.
— PRINCE WENZEL ANTON VON KAUNITZ, Austrian statesman

7

Two other bags were also missing. The bus driver had come from the restaurant in time to see a car speeding away, a car with an out-of-state license.

Once more I was back to wearing everything I owned. The new suit, shirts, underwear, all were gone. What money I had left was in my pocket but I would need clothing in which to work, toilet articles, a razor. It would not leave much.

Talking with a man on the bus gave me an idea. He lived in Barstow, California, and would be getting off there. He asked what work I had been doing, and I mentioned the assessment job in Arizona. He suggested there were several people in Barstow who had mining claims but no particular urge to do the required work. Most of the local laborers did not want to take a temporary job when they might miss out on something more permanent.

He named an attorney who had some claims and usually hired his work done, so when the bus reached Barstow, I got off. The attorney, whom I saw the next day, needed no work done, but he called an old man he knew who had claims and I made the connection.

He would drive me to the claims and show me

what needed to be done and, if all went well, would return and pick me up. If not, there was an old Model T there I could drive back to Barstow. "Ain't much of a road," he explained, "just wheeltracks, but you stick to it an' it will bring you right into town. Don't be misled by signs. Most of them just go to abandoned mines, or towns that ain't there anymore.

"The claims are in the Owl's Head Mountains, just over the ridge from Wingate Pass, to the south of Death Valley. Country's mighty dry out thataway but there's springs if you know where to find 'em."

He glanced at me out of the corners of his eyes. "You upset by rattlers, boy? There's a-plenty of them out there — ketched a sight of them in rat-traps. They crawl around at night, y'know.

"Never had no trouble with 'em myself. All a man's got to do is keep his eyes open. An' when you get up in the mornin', shake out your boots before you put 'em on. That's not for snakes. Centipedes, scorpions, tarantulas, and the like, they favor warm boots."

He drove on, winding along the sandy desert road. "There's two claims. Two hundred dollars. You will need the grub I got back here, fifty dollars' worth, an' I'll dee-duct for that.

"Ain't likely you'll see anybody. That there's mighty barren, empty country, but if you do, just tell 'em you're workin' for me. Ever'body out thataway knows me.

"Owl Holes will be your closest water unless

there's been rain. Brackish, but you can drink it. They're kind of south of the claims, maybe a mile or two, but I keep a barrel of water on the claim."

He indicated the trail we were driving. "This here road leads straight into town, like I said. Don't you go wanderin' off. Old mines out yonder where nobody's been in years — deathtraps, most of them.

"Over east a ways, in the Ivanpahs now, used to be some horse thieves yonder. May be there yet. I ain't lost nothin' there so I ain't looked, but they were bad ones, right bad.

"Mostly pick an' shovel work where we're goin'. Got some giant out there, giant powder, y' know. Never used it much, myself. You dig into the hillside where the tunnel is, an' you fix up the road. I won't ask anything more."

"What have you got out there?"

"Manganese. I don't have much know-how about anything but gold or silver, but there's a good prospect nigh to the Owl Holes. That's manganese, and an engineer I helped one time, he showed me this place where you're goin'. Lay claim to it, he said, an' hang on. Next time there's a war you'll be rich. Well, I'm hangin' on, but where's the war? Folks are just too darn peaceful these days."

He drove on in silence. Then he slowed for a dip in the road, scooted around a big rock that had been easier to avoid than move, and he said, "This here claim? She's cost me six, seven hundred dollars so far, but I sold a gold claim over on

Caliente Canyon for four thousand here a while back. Sell one once in a while."

"Ever think of working one yourself?"

"Work one? Hell, no, I find 'em. Takes money to turn a claim into a producer. Takes money, hope, an' faith, and I got none of them. I find myself a hole in the ground, some likely-lookin' ore, and I act kind of mysterious. I make sure any rock I show is good stuff, an' never tell where it comes from. If they're interested, I show 'em the hole and spec'late how there's millions in the hole, an' maybe there is if I can sell it for enough."

"Isn't that dishonest?"

"Maybe. I ain't a judge, anymore. Seems to me folks want something to hope for. They want to believe in something. Well, I give them hope, an' if they believe enough they have faith. What more can a man get out of life? Anyway, who knows? They might strike it rich."

"This claim we're going to now — is it one of those?"

"Not by a durned sight. This one is my hope, an' my faith. I got no faith in gold. I got no faith in silver. Manganese, that's a serious metal. I got faith in manganese."

It was a winding desert road, a good enough surface but with sandy stretches. The mountains were bare rock and when rain fell upon them it ran down into the sand and was lost. The area we crossed was scattered with dry lakes, or *playas*, as they are called, and along the alluvial fans there were scattered large boulders, gravel, and sand. The predominant plant was the creosote bush. From the air, or from high on a mountain, this plant can look to the uninitiated like an orchard, its growth is so regularly spaced. The struggle for what water falls is so great that the creosote roots poison any but a few plants that try to grow near it. This accounts for the open spaces around each creosote bush.

"See you got books along. Good idea. You do your work early, boy, or in the evenin'. Nobody in his right mind works in the noonday sun. You travel in the desert, you travel early an' late.

"Everything out there" — he gestured toward the desert — "is there because it learned how to survive. Lots of plants have hard surfaces on the top of the leaves, to reflect sunlight. Cactus grows with kinda fluted sides so's not to expose too much surface to the sun at one time.

"Kangaroo rats, now? They maybe never take a drink their life long. They get what moisture they need from what they eat."

He took a hand from the wheel to point off to our left. "Spring over yonder. Sets in a kind of box. Warm water, but good. You can drink it anytime.

"Paradise Spring, they call it. Named for a mine back yonder. I sure enough hope whoever found it found paradise, because from what I hear he didn't find much else. Some float, maybe.

"But that's just talk. I never worked that hole, know durned little about it.

87

"Ever hear of Shorty Harris? Folks always askin' about Death Valley Scotty. Know him well. He'd make three of Shorty Harris but wasn't half the man. Oh, Scotty was all right. Liked him. Shorty, he was kind of special. Didn't have an enemy in the world except hisself. Shorty had a nose for the rich stuff. He could find it better 'n anybody but, once he got some of it, drank and gambled until nothing was left.

"Then he'd get his old burro and head for the desert again. One time, Greenwater, I think it was, in Death Valley. Shorty and his partner found gold — gold so rich they could scarce believe it. Shorty, he would stake their claims and his partner would go to town and file on them.

"I know! You guessed it! Shorty's partner gets to town and he's thirsty. Also he's a talker. He gets a couple of belts of cactus juice and tells ever'body in the saloon what they found. They buy him drinks, get him drunk, he passes out and forgets to file, and all those men, they come streamin' out there, filin' on all the ground in sight. Shorty winds up with nothin'! Nothin' at all."

The old man swerved his car around a sand hill, dropped, bouncing, into a wash, and made a desperate dash up the other side, bouncing over rocks and dodging a near collision with an invading bunch of creosote.

"Shorty was a finder, not a keeper. Come from back east somewhere, New Jersey, I think it was, an' hoboed his way west when he was a youngster.

"Orphan. Least, that's what I heard. Died a few years back an' if what they say is true, he was buried standin' up in the lowest part of Death Valley.

"They were diggin' a grave but it was just too durned hot, so they stood the coffin on one end and filled it in. Buried him standin' up at the lowest part of Death Valley. Ol' Shorty would have loved that. Had his epitaph: *Here lies Shorty Harris, single-blanket jackass prospector,* or something like that. Never seen the spot, m'self."

We stopped at Garlic Spring to fill the radiator from a water trough. The spring itself was about a hundred yards up the draw, and when we started on I was telling myself that if I had to drive back alone I would hope the tire tracks would still be there, as roads or trails intersected with our road every mile or so.

The old man talked steadily, but everything he had to say was amusing or informative. He knew a lot about desert plants and talked of them. We were climbing slowly, headed for the Granite Mountains with the Avawatz showing up behind them.

It was all of seventy miles to the claim, and as much attention as I paid, I was to wish I had looked around still more.

The claim was nothing. Somebody had opened a tunnel and dug in a few feet. Some flimsy poles had been stuck in the ground and they supported a few sheets of metal that offered a little shade. There were a couple of barrels underneath, one containing water. There were several picks, a shovel, a single-jack, and some drills.

An old Model T with no top stood under the shed. "If something happens an' I don't get back in five days, you just wind up that ol' buggy an' drive her into town. Come to my place an' I'll pay you off.

"Work in the tunnel, yonder. Get in as far as you can in the time you've got, but if you run out of something to do of an evenin' you might walk back along the road an' roll some of those big rocks away."

He looked at me again, as if seeing me for the first time. "Think you can do it, boy?"

"No problem," I said, and meant it.

He let out the clutch and rolled away, making a quick turn to dodge a big rock. That was another case where I should have been paying more attention.

For a long time I just stood there, listening to the sound of the car for as long as I could hear it. He was an old man. Suppose he didn't make it back to Barstow?

Picking up my duffel, I walked back under the awning. It was late afternoon and the sun was under some rare clouds, very thin, very high.

There was a fire-ring of rocks and some piled wood alongside it. There was a coffeepot, a frying pan, some odds and ends of knives, forks, and enamel dishes. And suspended under the awning was a hammock.

I suppose I was lonely. I know that often I longed

for someone with whom I could talk of books, writers, and things of the mind, but that was not to be for a long time, except here and there when I chanced on some other lost literary soul. Loneliness is of many kinds, and the mere presence and companionship of people does not suffice. The people I had been meeting were friendly, pleasant, and the salt of the earth, but they did not speak my language. I enjoyed them, but something in me reached out for more. Moreover, I needed time to write, to sit down, free of care, and just write. So far I had been trying, here and there — aboard ship, at the mine, and elsewhere — but I needed more.

One is not, by decision, just a writer. One becomes a writer by writing, by shaping thoughts into the proper or improper words, depending on the subject, and by doing it constantly. There was so much I needed to learn that could only be learned by doing, by sitting down with a typewriter or a pen and simply writing. Most young writers waste at least three paragraphs and often three pages writing *about* their story rather than telling it. This was one of the many things I had yet to learn.

Behind every great piece of art, be it music, sculpture, poetry, architecture, painting, or literature, there is design, and so there must be, although every once in a while one will discover some critic speaking of a "formula" story, as if there were any other kind. In some stories it is not so easily discernible, but the design is there, and so it should be, as our predecessor Will Shakespeare knew so very well.

Too many books are written about writing by those who are not writers. Recently I read a book on how a certain great dramatist arrived at his dialogue, an account that would be amusing to any professional writer, it was so little based in fact.

Fortunately, I had slept in a hammock before this, so I managed very well. It at least kept me off the ground where I might awaken with a rattlesnake alongside me for warmth. As it was, two mornings later I shook a four-inch scorpion out of my boot.

The work before me was just what I had done before, although the ground in which I worked was softer, and also, I might add, dangerous as one penetrated deeper. Whoever followed me would need to use timber. As it was, I cut quite a bit from the hillside and then turned to the road, where much work needed to be done.

On the fourth day I had completed my work, yet I waited through the fifth, puttering about, straightening up, gathering the tools and gear together.

Having lost most of what I owned when my gear was taken from the bus, I had but two books. They had been left on the seat when I went into the café with the others, and the thieves had not been interested. One was Edith Wharton's *Ethan Frome*; the other, Donn Byrne's *Messer Marco Polo*.

The first I had read on the two evenings after

work when I first arrived. Now I completed Byrne's book, and when morning came I tossed my few belongings into the back of the old Model T.

Surprisingly, it started easily. I had wrestled with a crank before that, and had seen others do it, and expected trouble.

It started easily. The trouble came later.

8

But not much later. In driving away, the old man had made a quick turn to get around a rock, and that was what I should have remembered. At the last minute I did, but too late. The car went over the rock, dropped hard, and something broke.

The car would not move. I got out, walked around, and it was obvious even to me. The axle was broken, and the old Model T was going nowhere. I turned off the ignition, picked up my bundle from the car seat, and looked around.

It was not yet five o'clock in the morning, and I would be getting nowhere standing about bemoaning my luck. I had no canteen, no way in which to carry water. There was a can of pears left, so I put it in my bundle and started south. The first water would be at the Owl Holes roughly four miles from the claim.

Shouldering my bundle, I started off, walking steadily. That I was in trouble I had no doubt, but if the old man was coming for me, he would be driving right along the road by which we came in.

The air was still cool, but the day would be hot. I must begin looking for shade, a place to take shelter from the midday sun. Physically I was in good shape and had always done a lot of walking, so that part did not distress me. It was the lack of water that was important.

The road by which I had come trended southwest, then turned sharply back to the southeast, as I recalled. Among the springs mentioned on the way in, the old man had spoken of Drinkwater Spring, which was off the trail to the south, and there was a foot trail that led from there to the road by which we had come. If I dared chance it, that cutoff might save me several miles.

Near Drinkwater Spring there was an old cabin, so it might be a place to stop during the worst of the day's heat. My walking pace was roughly three miles an hour, and after a good long drink at the Owl Holes, I started down that road to the southwest, walking steadily.

It was a few minutes after six when I left the Owl Holes. I was guessing I could continue walking until ten o'clock, when it would be wise to find shade, if any, and wait out the day. In walking west I knew I would be walking parallel to the road that ran east, but cutting across country is dangerous, as one has no idea how many gullies one will have to climb into and out of. I held to the trail and the tracks of the old man's car.

It was flat desert, scattered with rocks and creosote. When I reached the turning point, I was feeling good and checked my time. The sky above was impossibly blue but that would not be for long. Soon the heat would turn it to brassy white and the sand beneath my feet would grow hot. I knew that temperatures at this time of year could run well over one hundred degrees in the shade, and there was no shade.

I did not worry. I did not think. I simply walked, putting one foot ahead of the other and holding my destination in mind.

Soon I would have the Granite Mountains to my south and the Avawatz to the north, both well back from the road on which I walked. The tracks of the old man's car, coming and going, were plainly visible. There were no other tracks.

Desert nights are cold, but with the coming of day the cold disappears quickly and the heat is with you until sundown.

My shirt was soaked with sweat from walking but it had a pleasant, cooling effect. At the point where I must turn to the footpath that led to Drinkwater Spring, I hesitated. Leaving a known road is always a risk, and moreover, if the old man was driving out today, he might well pass by while I was off the road. Nevertheless, the water was there and I needed water, desperately. As near as I could figure, the cutoff must be eight or nine miles until it intersected with the road on which I was traveling.

My situation was serious. I had no means by which to carry water, and irritably I thought back to so many movies where, when a canteen is empty, it is thrown away. I can think of nothing more incredibly stupid. If the man comes upon water, how will he carry it? Yet the scene is repeated over and over.

It was after eleven before I reached water. It was a small pipe leading from the spring to a trough in an old corral. Cupping my hands, I drank, and drank again. Then I splashed water on my face and on my shirt. The old cabin was not far off and I walked over, dropping down in the shade.

Grateful for the respite, I leaned my head back and slept. It was all of an hour before I awakened, and then only to move into deeper shade. After a bit I walked to the pipe from the spring and soaked up some more water.

Some blue quail came out of the brush and gathered around water trickling from the trough, and later a jack rabbit hopped slowly by, unaware of me, and obviously unafraid.

I slept again, awakened, drank, then dozed for a while. From time to time I glanced at my watch. I would wait until four, I told myself. If possible, I wanted to be back on the familiar road while it was still light. Otherwise I might miss it entirely.

At a rough guess I had covered something more than twenty miles that morning, but the worst stretch would be at the end.

Thinking of that, I bathed my feet in cool water from the trough, dried them, and prepared myself to move out. I had far to go and was impatient to get on with it. Despite that fact, I enjoyed my brief stop at Drinkwater Spring, and am sure had I stopped the night I would have seen some bighorns, for their tracks were all about. Obviously they watered here.

Beckoning signs invited me down all sorts of

roads. The signs to Randsburg made me hesitate. Was it close? But when I got there I would still be far from Barstow, where my payoff awaited me. Of course, I might hitch a ride into Barstow. Yet the only road I knew and the only one I could be sure of was the one I was following.

Now, having spent much time in the Mohave and Colorado Deserts, I know what my options were, yet given the circumstances, I probably did the right thing. At the moment I could not be sure.

Shouldering my small pack, I set out along the dim trail that should intersect with the road I needed, and roughly two hours later, it did.

If I recalled correctly, and I had learned to pay attention, the road that lay ahead was not only straight but flat, hard-packed sand for the most part, and at least ten miles to Garlic Spring. With luck I could make it during the cool hours of the night. By day that road would be pure hell. Temperatures in September often soared as high as 120 degrees, and down there on the desert flat where my feet were, it would be even hotter. Already that day I had walked farther at one stretch than ever before in my life, although days would come when I would walk much farther.

When I reached the main trail and started south for Garlic, a lot of the spring had gone from my step. The sun dropped from sight beyond the western mountains and the air grew cool. I walked steadily, only at a slower pace.

The stars appeared, incredibly bright in that

clear, cloudless desert air. Constantly I looked for some rock large enough to sit down upon, but saw nothing. Getting up from the ground would not be easy, so I hesitated, at that time, to attempt it. I was very much afraid that if I sat down I would not have the strength to get up.

On I walked. Occasionally I sang, which was enough to protect me from anything predatory. The only persons who ever enjoyed my singing were myself and my kids, before they became old enough to know better.

Crossing an old desert road that came in from out of nowhere, I came upon a collection of broken wood that might have been the tailgate of a truck. There was other debris around, too, and so I stopped, gathered sticks together, and built a fire. What the hour was I no longer remember, but it was probably about 2:00 A.M. It was cold — cold as only the desert can be where there is nothing to hold the heat of the day. I dug out a hollow for my hips and settled down beside my small fire to rest, and sleep.

Wind rustled the brush, stirring mysteriously in the smaller plants, rattling seedpods still clinging from another year. I did not remove my boots. If my feet should swell, as they almost surely would, I would not get my boots on again.

In the first faint blue light of dawn, with stars still hanging in the sky, I awakened, shaking with chill. My small supply of fuel was gone, so I tightened my bootlaces and started walking myself warm.

It actually felt good to be moving, but I was worried. The terrain ahead was flat and offered no promise of shelter from the sun when day came. Yet there was a black shadow ahead and slightly to my left, and I remembered that near Garlic Spring were the Tiefort Mountains, such as they were, so there might be a chance of some hole I could crawl into out of the sun.

At Garlic Spring, I opened my can of pears. They were half pears and I took them into my mouth, holding them as long as I could before they gradually almost melted away. I sat on the ground, resting and taking my time with the pears.

A good third of the can was juice, for which I was grateful, and I took my time with that, too, and carried the empty can with me when I walked away. A sign near the spring warned me it was more than thirty-five miles to Barstow. Before leaving the spring I filled the can with water. It was difficult to carry but might help a little, yet when I had walked only a short distance I saw among the scattered rocks two that had fallen together to make a small cave, open on both sides. Carrying my can of water, I went down over the rocks and crawled in out of the sun.

It was early to stop, yet thirty-five miles without more water than I had, on the open desert, was insanity. I would simply wait out the day and try to make most of that distance during the night to come.

Hunched in my small shelter I leaned a shoulder against the brown rock and tried to sleep. From time to time I sipped water from the pear can.

The cool hours of morning slipped easily away and it became hot. Suddenly, my eye detected movement. At the back opening of my shelter was a stretch of baked white earth and crossing it toward me was a good-sized desert rattler, obviously heading for the shade I occupied. He was still some distance off, so I gathered a handful of sand and threw it at him.

He stopped, head up, tongue flicking. I threw another handful and he coiled but did not rattle. It was still not hot enough to kill him out there, but soon would be, and a rattlesnake cannot stand long exposure to the hot sun.

I threw another handful with some larger rocks this time, and he came out of his coil and started to crawl away. Satisfied that he was no longer planning to share my shade, I let him go.

Nothing else stirred. It was a long, slow morning and afternoon. I dozed, awakened, dozed again. My ears were always attuned to the hoped-for sound of a motor, but luck failed me, as it often has. In the distance, down the way I would go, but probably farther out, I could see a brief shower falling, a rarity at that time of year. Several times I saw dust-devils, those miniature desert whirlwinds that spring up suddenly, travel briefly, then die.

Somewhere along the line I fell asleep and slept as if drugged, awakened only when the coolness began to come. It was after 5:00 P.M. when I refilled my can at the spring and started once again.

The water at Garlic Spring had not been particularly good, but it was water. The only other water I knew of was Paradise Spring, which the old man had mentioned, and it was more than a mile off the road, which meant perhaps three miles extra added to my hike.

Was it worth it? I did not know.

And what had happened to the old man? Suppose he had died? Would I ever get paid?

The night was cool, and I walked steadily. I was very tired, and occasionally I stumbled. The road turned left down a wash and followed it for a short distance. It was an effort to climb out. I sipped a little of my water and decided I had to make the side trip to Paradise Spring. It was in a box, he'd said, set down in a patch of grass.

Finishing the little water I carried, I refilled at Paradise Spring, but by the time I got back to the road I was dead tired. I sat down on a low bank of sand piled by the wind around some brush. How long I sat there I do not know, but the realization that I must get as far as possible before the sun came up got me started.

My mouth was dry, my lips cracked. My face felt hot despite the coolness of the night. As I had on several previous occasions, I put a pebble in my mouth to ease my thirst.

A few miles farther along I finished the little water in the can and must have dropped it. That I do not remember. I do remember sipping some milky water from a rut in the road, probably left by that brief shower I had seen from a distance.

The town was suddenly there, and I remember crossing a bridge into town and walking up the street to a café. I dropped down on a stool and asked for a Coke.

The waitress said, "Man, you look like you've been through it. What happened?"

The Coke bottle felt cold and wonderful in my hand and there was ice in the glass. "I just walked in from Death Valley," I said.

A man on a stool near me turned and stared. "You walked in? You got to be crazy."

When I found him, the old man was ill, sick in bed, but his daughter paid me the $150.

"Sorry, boy, I'm real sorry. Planned on pickin' you up."

I explained about the car. "Well, she's no loss. Never was much account, anyway."

My next stop was Los Angeles, and then San Pedro and a ship.

An idea upon which attention is peculiarly concentrated is an idea which tends to realize itself.

— CHARLES BAUDOUIN

9

When first I arrived in Los Angeles, I was hitch-hiking a ride on a truck. By the time I bought a suit of clothes and other necessaries, there was not too much money left. No doubt I should have begun hunting a job at once, but I was hungry for books, anxious to be learning, so I rented a room in a small hotel close to the library and divided my time between it and the shelves of second-hand bookstores close by.

In those days one could buy a meal ticket, which was punched out as you ate, and I bought two. First, I attempted to get a job on a newspaper, but I had no experience and had not graduated from any school, so I got nowhere. A few attempts in other directions were equally unsuccessful. Many commented that they were laying off help rather than hiring.

Browsing through the shelves in bookstores or libraries, I was completely happy, dipping into a book here, another there, tasting, savoring, learning. Many books I would not read for years I first examined at this time.

On the Death Valley claim I had read Byrne's *Messer Marco Polo*, a very pleasant little book but not at all what I wanted. It was years later that

I found it, and years more before I owned it, but what I really wanted was the two-volume work on Polo with notes by Cordier and Yule, which far surpassed anything else in the field. That book was to lead me to Yule's *Cathay and the Way Thither*, which was a real joy.

It would be impossible for me to explain my early fascination with Asia, although it could well have sprung from reading a child's version of *The Arabian Nights*. Years later, when I acquired the full set in the Sir Richard Burton translation, I was content that I had the best. Burton's knowledge of the Arabic language, of the customs and mores of Near Eastern and African peoples, made his comments and notes a rich entertainment and an introduction to many aspects of the life not touched upon elsewhere. The only comparable collection, of similar but different stories, is *The Ocean of Story* in the Penzer and Tawney edition.

Although known as the "Arabian Nights," the stories largely originated in India or farther east, as did those in *The Ocean of Story*. Many of the places can readily be identified by anyone with a sailing knowledge of Asiatic waters. No matter what the content of the stories, the locales were invariably actual places, just as in my own stories.

We in the Western world have been so involved with seafaring in the Mediterranean and Atlantic that we have almost ignored what was happening on the other side of the world, when much longer voyages were being made and another part of the world explored.

When Vasco da Gama arrived in the harbors of India after his long voyage around the Cape of Good Hope, he found those harbors crowded with shipping.

Almost two thousand years earlier, when Nearchus, Alexander the Great's admiral, was looking for a pilot for the Indian Ocean and Persian Gulf, he had no trouble at all in finding one. Ships from China had come to Babylon in the time of Nabonidus, and before Columbus discovered America, Cheng Ho had sailed back from Africa with a giraffe for the Emperor's zoo.

Ships were sailing from the south of India for Madagascar and Africa over an open ocean of more than two thousand miles. The area now known as Indonesia had been explored and colonies established, at least one in Borneo, by the ninth century.

It was about this time that I read *Quentin Durward* by Sir Walter Scott and *Ivory Apes and Peacocks* by James Huneker, and followed it with *Iconoclasts* by the same author.

I was in the habit of listing books read, even then, but often lost the lists, so the only ones intact are from periods after 1930.

At the end of a week in Los Angeles, I gathered my gear and headed for San Pedro and the sea again.

Arriving at San Pedro, I registered at the Marine Service Bureau for a ship, discovering it might be as much as three months before my number came up. At that time the West Coast ships were unionized but East Coast ships were not, and conditions aboard ship were drastically different. On the West Coast the food was better, the fo'c'sles cleaner, and conditions generally much better. As a result, many seamen wanted to ship off the West Coast, and at the time I arrived it was said there were seven hundred seamen "on the beach" in San Pedro.

At the time the most important place to many seamen on the beach was the Seaman's Church Institute, a place where one could pick up mail, where there was a game room, a small reading room and library, and a place where one could shower, shave, and clean up. They also had a dormitory where clean beds were available. I've forgotten the price, which I rarely had, but it was fifty cents or a dollar.

On Wednesday nights there was entertainment in the game room, offered by some amateur or semiprofessional group, followed by volunteer acts from among the seamen, which was invariably the best part.

A surprising number of seafaring men have at one time or another worked in some phase of the theater. Some were not good enough for the big time and for one reason or another dropped out and went to sea. Others had become alcoholics or gotten themselves in trouble otherwise.

Several men I knew had played the vaudeville circuits, but movies were replacing them in many theaters and the sea no doubt seemed an escape.

In any event, during my short time in San Pedro, I saw some very entertaining acts.

Of course, it was to the reading room that I went. They had three or four hundred books, if I recall correctly, varied in quality but all interesting. Perhaps a third of them were nonfiction.

Finding work was almost out of the question with so many skilled seamen standing by and ready to work, yet occasionally there was something. My first dollar was earned helping a man unload a truck. A week later I picked up two days of rough-painting in the shipyards, and that job got me into a couple of days bucking rivets.

What money I earned was necessary for eating. I slept in empty boxcars, on piles of lumber, anywhere out of the rain and wind. By day, when not working, or during the evenings, I read.

The first book, a real delight, was *The Expedition of Humphry Clinker* by Tobias Smollett. I had heard of Smollett but this was the first book of his that I'd read, and I enjoyed every line. I also read *The Bar Sinister* by Richard Harding Davids, a story about a dog, and a good yarn. Another great dog story was *The Call of the Wild* by Jack London.

There was a copy of *Knight on Seamanship* in the library and I studied it when I could get my hands on it, as several others were reading it too.

It was a rough time on the waterfront. The Pacific fleet was located at San Pedro then and the town swarmed with sailors ashore, most of whom went on to Los Angeles on the big red cars of the Pacific Electric. Under a trestle of the P.E., the longshoremen had a crap game going almost continually.

With the mixture of nationalities that made up the American Merchant Marine, there was sure to be friction. Rough-and-tumble fights were common. As long as the watching crowd did not block traffic and no local citizen was involved, the police rarely interfered, enjoying the fight as much as any other spectators. When Fitzgerald, a Liverpool-Irish oiler, whipped Frisco Brady on the corner of Front and Fourth, there were at least four policemen among the spectators. The fight, a brutal, battering match, lasted upwards of forty minutes.

Waterfront fighting has nothing to do with rules or sportsmanship, only with winning. Dead Man's Island, which at the time still marked the entrance to the ship channel, caught the drifting body of more than one loser. However, that was not the reason for its name. Various stories are told but the one sure to be true was told by Hugo Reid, who probably knew as much about what was happening in Southern California as anyone.

Captain William Mervine, with a party of sailors, attacked Captain Flores and a party of "insurgents" on the Dominguez rancho. Six men were killed, six wounded. Mervine buried the American sailors on the lonely little island in San Pedro Bay. The battle had taken place on October 8, 1846, as the United States was in the process of acquiring California.

Dead Man's Island was finally removed as a

menace to navigation.

Today, a collection of shops and restaurants in San Pedro is known as Ports o' Call, and it occupies the site of the old E. K. Wood Lumber Dock, where lumber schooners from Aberdeen, Coos Bay, and other points on the Northwest Coast used to discharge their cargoes of raw lumber for the building of Los Angeles. There were several slips and each one was usually occupied by such a vessel. They were old and battered, built only for the carrying of lumber. Their crews were usually Swedes or Norwegians, big, husky men who worked cargo as well as working as seamen.

The discharged lumber was usually piled on the dock awaiting shipment by train, and the rails ran right up to the dock. Perhaps they ran out on the docks — I do not clearly remember.

However, what was important to me was that often, in piling great stacks of planks, there would be spaces left like caves where a man could crawl in out of the rain. If he was thoughtful enough to provide himself with a newspaper he could wrap around his body under his coat, he might sleep there out of the rain and in reasonable comfort. I use the last term in a relative sense. What is comfort to some is cruel hardship to others.

This might be a good place to add that I had a family, including two brothers and a sister, but they were living their own lives, with problems of their own. I was going the way I had chosen, with no intention of leaning upon anyone for sustenance. My parents knew where I was but not how I was surviving.

It was at this time that I read Boswell's *The Life of Samuel Johnson, Ll.D.*, without doubt one of the greatest biographies in the English language. It was a book I read slowly, often returning to reread parts of it. I could not accept the generally believed idea that Boswell was merely someone who followed the great man about, duly noting his comments and ideas. The writing was too good, the appreciation of his subject too great. History was, of course, to bear me out, but many of the Boswell papers had not yet come to light or been published. I now have the complete set in my own library and have drawn upon them from time to time when picturing the London taverns and inns of the period. Samuel Pepys has proved another good source on the life of English public houses. Their periods of history are separated by just enough time to give one a fairly adequate picture of where men were going and what was happening in seventeenth- and eighteenth-century England.

Such books offer a valuable insight into social life as well as traveling conditions, the food being eaten, and what was imbibed in the taverns.

In re-creating the life of a time, it has always been my way to find the best possible sources — first person, if possible. There are many books of memoirs written by travelers, soldiers, sailors, merchants, and others which, if sought out, offer excellent pictures of their times.

One that I have found valuable as well as interesting is *The Memoirs of Vincent Nolte*, which was also one of the source books for Hervey Allen's *Anthony Adverse*, the first book I ever reviewed. The review was written for the *Sunday Oklahoman* of Oklahoma City when Professor Kenneth C. Kaufman was the book editor.

The Seamen's Institute was an education in itself, and some of the most remarkable characters I have ever known I first met there. One, whom we called Old Doc Yak after a comic-strip character of the time, inspired a short story I was to write and publish many years later. Another story of mine grew out of the checkers games that were a regular feature of the place.

There was an old longshoreman who came nearly every night to play. He was a thorough student of the game and had memorized all the plays in the books. He played using bottle tops for his "men" and disdained any but a few who had proved themselves able to give him a contest. One of these was Oriental Slim, a particular friend of mine. Another was a marine engineer. Either of these might beat him on occasion, but the occasions were rare.

Then came Sleeth, a slim, dark man with a fantastic head for figures. I've seen him stand beside the tracks and memorize the numbers on the boxcars as they rolled by, and be able to repeat them in order. They always checked out.

Sleeth was ignored at first when he suggested a game with the old man, but after he beat Oriental Slim, he was considered a likely candidate. What followed was cruel, although not intentionally so.

Checkers was more than a game to the old long-shoreman. It was his life, his very reason for being, and he was proud of his skill. Each move was studied with care and made only after much thought. Sleeth would carry on a conversation with bystanders, and as soon as the old man had made his move, he would, with scarcely a glance at the board, make his move.

And he would win every time.

Perhaps the sudden moves shook the old man's confidence. Perhaps the conversation did. After a few such games, the old man did not come back to the Seamen's Institute. Sleeth, like most of us, was a bird of passage, and soon he was gone too.

Often I would sit by the window in the game room and watch them, these men who came and went to and from all the seaports of the world. Every one was a character, and every one had a story. Some day I would write some of those stories, but at the time I was just another seaman on the beach, waiting for a ship.

And then one morning about four o'clock, I shipped off the dock on a freighter bound for the Far East. I took what used to be called, in sailing-ship days, a "pier-head jump," signing on in the First Mate's quarters by a dim light over his desk.

Back in the reading room of the Seamen's Institute, I left a couple of good books unfinished.

10

Unfortunately, in most of our schools the history of Europe and North America is taught as if it were the history of the world. The rest of the world is referred to only when Europeans or Americans were invading or trading. There has recently been a small change for the better but not nearly enough.

Not long ago, a distinguished historian was speculating on why all the great voyages of discovery began in Europe — which, of course, is not at all true. However, aside from the Viking voyages, which explored northern waters, most European exploratory ventures were toward the Far East.

The reasons were obvious. The riches of the Indies were known and had been known for centuries, and everybody was striving for easier access or a route they could control. Europe wanted the silks and spices of Asia, while Europe had nothing at all Asia wanted. Europe's only exportable item at the time was religion, and Asia certainly did not lack for religions of her own.

The fact of the matter is that Asiatic waters had been explored very thoroughly by her own people, and a lively trade was conducted from northern China to Africa and all points between, often with larger ships than any sailing European waters. The

Buddhist *Jatakas* speak of many voyages, and although the stories of Sinbad are fabulous, in many cases the islands and ports in his stories can be identified.

During the Vietnam War era, people were led into all sorts of foolishness by simple ignorance of a part of the world strange to them. Many believed that North and South Vietnam were one country divided, but such was never the case except briefly under French administration.

North Vietnam had originally been two countries, Annam and Tonkin, and their civilization derived largely from China. South Vietnam had formerly been known as Champa, and, like Cambodia's, its civilization came from India. Before France moved into the situation, the two countries had been fighting for nearly two thousand years.

Champa had always been a rich agricultural region, its bountiful crops a challenge to less fertile northern countries. Both Annam and Tonkin, usually with assistance from China, had attempted to dominate Champa. The Vietnam War was simply another move in the same continuing effort.

A very good book on the history of the area is D.G.E. Hall's *A History of South-east Asia*, although there are a number of other good ones.

Acquiring an education has many aspects, of which school is only one, and the present approach is, I believe, the wrong one. Without claiming to have all the answers, I can only express my feeling that our methods of instruction do much to hamper a child in learning. Our approach is pedestrian. We teach a child to creep when he should be running; education becomes a task rather than excitement. Yet each of us can remember one or two teachers who made learning an adventure, which it surely is.

Personally, I believe children should be taught to see, to observe, and to subject what they have seen to analysis, and this in the earliest grades. Very young children will often learn a difficult subject easily unless someone tells them it is "hard." To me it also seems obvious that a child should be taught some methods of reasoning, methods of scientific investigation. Children have an innate feeling for logic and, given the opportunity, would learn quickly.

Such instruction would be unthinkable in any country not a democracy, and if carried out in a democracy it might clear the air of a lot of loose thinking, loose public speaking, and the kind of questionable statements that fill the air during political and other campaigns. The first generation of parents who had such children would have a difficult time but would find their own thinking undergoing drastic change.

We do not at present educate people to think but, rather, to have opinions, and that is something altogether different. Many of the political ideas that have disturbed the world in the past fifty years could not exist in such an atmosphere.

Often I am asked if I would recommend my way of learning to others. I certainly would not.

A young man once asked me that question and I told him that the first time he read fifty nonfiction books for fun, in one year, he could think about it. Most students require the disciplined atmosphere, the academic setting, and the guidance a good school can offer. The association and exchange of ideas are important also.

My way was suited to me. I have never been very good at taking instruction. I enjoy lectures, and have attended many, but mostly I prefer the quiet of a library and the freedom to go off in any direction that pleases me.

What I have learned is only a modest amount of what I should like to have learned, and I have read few books that I could not read again with profit, but there have been only a few to which I have returned.

I have never had to strive to graduate, never to earn a degree. The only degrees I have are honorary, and I am proud to have them. I studied purely for the love of learning, wanting to know and understand. For a writer, of course, everything is grist for the mill, and a writer cannot know too much. Sooner or later everything he does know will find its uses.

A writer's brain is like a magician's hat. If you're going to get anything out of it, you have to put something in first.

I have studied a thousand things I never expected to use in a story, yet every once in a while these things will find a place.

I have read because I loved reading, and I have

learned because I loved learning, yet all one needs cannot come from books. It can come from sounds, from music, from the play of light and shadow, from the people one meets or those one does not meet.

Much of my background reading has been in diaries written by westward-moving people, or in memoirs by people from this country and others. What I want to know is how people were living, what they were thinking, how they expressed themselves. One problem with some recent western movies is that the writer or director has tried to impose a late-twentieth-century viewpoint on a nineteenth-century situation, and it won't work. A person or a situation can only be understood against the background of its own time.

One of the best pieces of writing about the American frontier is Stephen Vincent Benét's poem *The Ballad of William Sycamore*. His *American Names* is another good example, the poem ending with that beautiful line which has since been used as a book title, "Bury my heart at Wounded Knee."

Benét is, without doubt, one of the very best American writers, best known perhaps for his *John Brown's Body*, but many of his short stories about America and elsewhere cannot be surpassed. For example, "The Devil and Daniel Webster," "A Tooth for Paul Revere," and "Johnny Pye and the Fool-Killer" capture a wonderful mood of a time now gone, which he invests with a quality all his own. Another Benét story, *The Last Legion*, tells of a time in ancient Britain when the legions of Rome were finally leaving that island, abandoning it to the invading barbarians.

William Rose Benét, who wrote much fine poetry (and was brother to Stephen), is responsible for a great favorite of mine, a poem I often read to my children, "The Skater of Ghost Lake." His *Merchants from Cathay* is a delight.

Another favorite poem is Edwin Arlington Robinson's "Mr. Flood's Party." This one I also often recited, after learning it by many rereadings. One must understand when I speak of reciting that I was doing this around campfires, in bunkhouses, and such places. I have no skills at performance, only a good memory. Such audiences are not inclined to be critical, but I often found a high level of appreciation among them, and many times requests would be made for poems by Wordsworth, Byron, or Tennyson, to name only a few.

Wandering men have always had a love for poetry, perhaps in part because it can be easily memorized and provide company on many a cold and lonely night. Wars also give birth to poetry written by the combatants, and the sale of poetry books goes up during most wars.

Often when standing lookout in the ship's bow, I whiled away the time by repeating poetry that I had learned back along the way or, even more often, trying to compose some of my own. At the time I knew nothing of the various verse forms and would not have recognized an iambic pentameter if we had come face to face on the street.

All I had going for me at the time was a feeling for rhythm and a love for words.

The writing of poetry is rarely an easy thing, although once in a while everything will fall into place. Poe, I believe, needed four years to complete the final version of "The Raven." Of course, he was doing much else at the time. Goethe's *Faust* was begun in 1808; the second part did not appear until 1832.

When I first began writing and was unable to sell a short story, I wrote anything I could sell for a few dollars: two-line jokes, jingles, small bits of poetry or verse, mostly nature pieces. But those days were still far off and away when I shipped out of San Pedro for the Far East.

The roads to knowledge are many. One of the greatest for me began in a very unexpected way. We were coming up to the mouth of a jungle river and there were scattered islets in the approaches. On one of these I saw what appeared to be an interesting ruin and later, when I had some time, I hired a boy with a boat to sail me out there.

The ruin was not interesting, but the boy was. He wore a turban, a *baju* (short jacket), and a sarong, and was, he told me, an Arab.

Surprised, I asked him how an Arab happened to be in what was then the East Indies and is now Indonesia. He gave me an odd look, then replied that Arabs had been in those islands for four hundred years. Determined to overcome my ignorance (which was probably shared by many educated

Westerners), I plied him with questions. He could answer only a few, but he had opened wide a door that never closed and led to years of exciting reading and much speculation.

Nobody aboard ship knew anything about the settlement of this part of the world, until one night at the wheel I mentioned it to the Second Mate. He remembered a book on the subject by an author named Warmington. Years later I found the book and it now sits on the shelves of my library.

I think the greatest gift anyone can give to another is the desire to know, to understand. Life is not for simply watching spectator sports, or for taking part in them; it is not for simply living from one working day to the next. Life is for delving, discovering, learning. Today, one can sit in the comfort of his own home and explore any part of the world or even outer space through books. They are all around us, offering such riches as can scarcely be believed. Also, I might add, having done both, it is better to sit in comfort with a cold drink at hand and read the tale than to actually walk out of the Mohave Desert as I did.

The armchair adventurer has all the advantages, believe me. As I have said elsewhere, and more than once, I believe adventure is nothing but a romantic name for trouble.

What people speak of as adventure is something nobody in his right mind would seek out, and it becomes romantic only when one is safely at home. It is much better to watch someone riding a camel across a desert on a movie screen than it is to be up on the camel's back, traveling at a pace of two and a half to three miles per hour through a blazing hot day with the sand blowing.

A beachcomber we picked up in Shanghai, as we were short of hands, a man we knew as Russian Joe Smith (though I don't believe he was Russian, Joe, or Smith), proved unexpectedly helpful. He had come aboard with some of his gear and I was showing him where he would bunk and telling him a little about the setup. He noticed some books on my bunk and asked, "What's them?"

"Just some stuff I've been reading," I told him.

"You like books? I'll bring you some."

To be honest, I was not expecting much, as Joe was obviously a rough character whose reading was probably confined to the sports pages or crime news of the daily paper, yet I was surprised when he showed up with two well-worn volumes by George Borrow, *Lavengro* and *Romany Rye*. The two books are an account of Borrow's time among the Gypsies and what he learned there, and I was delighted.

"There's more," he said. "Once I leave they're for grabs."

Smith's story was a sordid one. He had jumped ship at Taku Bar in northern China, and had been on the beach there as well as in Shanghai. In the latter place he had picked up an alcoholic woman in a bar and she had taken him home. Apparently they had cared for each other for several months.

125

She was an educated, intelligent woman whose husband, distressed by her drinking, had gone away into western China with no intention of returning. He had taken everything but about thirty books. Just one week before I met Joe, she had died, and her relatives showed up, ordering Joe off the premises. As it happened, he had paid her rent for the past two months. So he simply gathered everything of hers that was worth anything and left.

"Had money coming to her," Joe said. "They couldn't have cared less while she was alive." He glanced at me. "She was too good a woman for me, educated and all that, but she liked me an' I took care of her."

"Were you working? How did you pay the rent?"

"Panhandled. You ask a man for the price of a meal in Shanghai and he's so surprised to see an American on his uppers that he'll give you fifty bucks, maybe. I know guys on the beach here who can panhandle enough in one day to keep them drunk for a month.

"All the jobs I could do were done cheaper by the Chinese, but I didn't want to leave her, she being alone like that.

"I'm goin' back one more time and I'll bring some of those books."

When he returned he brought twelve books, all he could carry with his own gear. Of the dozen, I recall but three titles: *The Harvester* by Gene Stratton Porter; *To Have and to Hold* by Mary

Johnston; and one I have read several times since, and which for me was a real discovery.

It was *Lord Jim* by Joseph Conrad.

Whoever would make of himself a distinctive individual must be keen to perceive what he is not.

— Friedrich Schleiermacher

11

Only one who has learned much can fully appreciate his ignorance.

He knows so well the limits of his knowledge and how much lies waiting to be learned.

What had men thought? What had men believed? How did they come by those thoughts and beliefs? How had men learned to govern themselves? Were the processes the same everywhere?

Did man build cities because of an inner drive, like that of the beaver to build dams? How much of what we do is free will, and how much programmed in our genes? Why is each people so narrow that it believes that it, and it alone, has all the answers? In religion, is there but one road to salvation? Or are there many, all equally good, all going in the same general direction?

I have read my books by many lights, hoarding their beauty, their wit or wisdom against the dark days when I would have no book, nor a place to read.

I have known hunger of the belly kind many times over, but I have known a worse hunger: the need to know and to learn.

Once, when hitchhiking, I was picked up by a professor from some small college. He noticed

I carried a book in my coat pocket, and was curious. It was a Modern Library edition, in the limp bindings they used to have, which sold at the time for 95 cents. This one contained Nietzsche's *Ecce Homo*, and *The Birth of Tragedy*.

The professor was a pedantic man of limited imagination and seemed almost offended that I was reading such a book. (I suspected after a few minutes' conversation that he had not read it himself.) He plied me with questions. Obviously I did not fit some category in which he decided I belonged, and when he dropped me off in town, I suspect he was relieved to be rid of me.

He kept asking me why I wanted to read such a book. At first, he doubted I was reading it. Where had I heard of Nietzsche?

When I told him I thought it was in the preface to a book on Schopenhauer, he was even more disturbed and probably believed I was lying. Fortunately, there seem to be few of his kind, and my subsequent friendships with university professors have proved exciting, stimulating, and fun. Perhaps I was fortunate in that the first group I met was at the University of Oklahoma in the 1930's. At that time I met Kenneth C. Kaufman, Ben Botkin, Walter Stanley Campbell (who also wrote as Stanley Vestal), Carl Coke Rister, Paul Sears, and others. Sears had just written *Deserts on the March*, one of the very first books on ecology, when that word was scarcely known. I believe also that the book was the first best seller to come from a university press. Stuart Chase followed it a bit later with *Rich Land, Poor Land*, also on the subject, in 1936.

Having been over a lot of country I had seen what was happening to the land, and was pleased to get a chance to review Sears's book for a farm magazine. Ecology had been getting into some of my stories, principally one titled "Merrano of the Dry Country." It appeared in a pulp magazine and dealt not only with proper usage of the land but with the race question. That story first appeared about forty years ago, or a bit more.

The lists of books I read in my earlier years have largely been lost, but my memory for some is clear. It was a knockabout time for me: of going to sea, working in mines, lumber camps, and sawmills, doing whatever was available to make an honest dollar. Many of the activities of young men of the time I missed entirely, or in part. Either I was working, traveling from one place to another, or else I did not have the money to afford it.

At the time I thought that I might make a career of fighting. My early training had been good, and in knocking about the country I had picked up a few dollars here and there in small-town boxing rings. For that reason, among others, I never smoked and rarely had a drink. The idea that it might be fun to get drunk never appealed to me, for I had come to believe I could cope with any situation that might arise if I had my wits about me. There was one night in Shanghai when I was in more trouble than one man could handle. Three drunken British sailors pitched in to help, and help they did, but at bitter cost to themselves. Had they been sober, with the right coordination and reflexes, I think they would have made it.

Several times while traveling in Asia I hired students to read sight translations of books unavailable, so far as I knew, in English. On occasion this took place on a riverbank. Several times it was in coffee- or teahouses, where we never failed to pick up an interested audience. In one case a rather violent argument developed between the reader and a listener over a line from an Indian poet, Bhartrihari. I thought the Indus River was about to flow with fresh blood, but after a good deal of shouting and waving of arms and flashing eyes, the listener strode away. When he was well out of hearing, my reader said, "He may be right, at that."

(It was Bhartrihari, incidentally, who said of a woman: "She talks to one man, looks at a second, and thinks of a third.")

One book always led to another and occasionally my discoveries led to a whole succession of books, but there was no intent in my reading except to learn and to know. Later, when I actually began doing research on various eras of history, from curiosity or because of something I wished to write, all that changed.

I read *Crime and Punishment* while in Klamath Falls, Oregon. I had heard much of Dostoevsky but was surprised by this book — surprised and very impressed. Several times I turned back to reread sections of the book. At the time I was working in a sawmill, off-bearing on the green chain. And that, my friends, is purely hard work.

When a log is cut into planks, those planks (in this case three inches thick and twelve inches wide) are green, fresh-cut lumber, and heavy. One takes a plank from the chain and puts it aboard a truck standing nearby. Meanwhile, the chain from the saw is bringing more planks, and more and more. If one is strong, reasonably agile, and gets his timing right, he can put in an eight-hour shift without too much trouble, but for hours at a stretch those planks keep coming. That is one description of off-bearing on the green chain.

(It has been years since I have been in a sawmill, and it is probably all done by machinery now, as are most of the jobs I used to do. I feel very sorry indeed for any young man without an education in these days, for there is literally nowhere to go.)

Also while on that job I read *The Moonstone* by Wilkie Collins, as well as *Plain Tales from the Hills* and *Kim* (for the second time), both by Kipling.

We hear a lot of talk these days about violence, but we forget the many generations that have grown up on stories of violence. The bloodiest of all, perhaps, were the so-called fairy tales, but I would have missed none of them and doubt if I did, yet I see little difference between Jack killing a fabled giant and Wyatt Earp shooting it out with an outlaw.

It often appears that violence is bad unless it is cloaked with enough tradition. There is much violence in the Bible, and the story could have been told in no other way. Many of Shakespeare's plays end with nearly everybody killed or dead by suicide. If we were to eliminate violence from our reading, we would have to eliminate all history, much of the world's great drama, as well as the daily newspaper.

What many people do not understand is that a child in growing up repeats within his early years much of the life history of man upon the earth, and it is necessary that he or she do this to become a human being.

At first a baby is simply a small animal that eats and sleeps, but there will come a time when he will want to build a shelter, to find some place he can crawl into, even if it is only a blanket over a chair or a table. Then there will be a time when the child plays capture games, wants a bow and arrow or perhaps a spear or other weapon. By acting out those early years of mankind's history, children put that history behind them. Most violent criminals are cases of arrested development where, for one reason or another, they never grow out of that period.

A girl, of course, will play with dolls, playing at being a mother, making a home, and what goes with it. All this is an essential part of growing up, of learning to be a human.

Much of this early violence can be sublimated through reading. In my own stories, there is no violence for the sake of violence. I tell it as it happened and my books are all thoroughly grounded in history. What so many of us who abhor violence often forget is that we have peace and civilized lives because there were men and women who went before us who were willing to fight for our freedom to live in peace.

It is always well to remember that many of us sleep safe at night because there are people out there cruising the streets and on call to keep it so. As many have discovered, violence is with us still, and no one is immune to a sudden strike in the night.

One of the questions a writer is most often asked is "Where do you get your ideas?" If a person does not have ideas, he had better not even think of becoming a writer. But ideas are everywhere. There are ideas enough in any daily newspaper to keep a man writing for years. Ideas are all about us, in the people we meet, the way we live, the way we travel, and how we think about things. It's important to remember that we are writing about people. Ideas are important only as they affect people. And we are writing about emotion. A few people reason, but all people feel.

The raw material is not important. It is what the writer does with the material. One writer will make you laugh, another can make you cry, and a third might write a horror story.

At least once a week I get a letter from someone who has material he wants me to shape into a story (wanting, of course, a piece of the action). But a writer builds a readership because those readers like what he does with a story, not because of the material.

There are only a certain number of plots, and they are very basic. When Ray Long was editor of *Cosmopolitan* years ago, he gave the same plot to six different writers, and they came up with six vastly different stories.

Plots are nothing devious. I have heard some literary or dramatic critics talk of plot in ways that indicated they had no grasp of the idea at all. A plot is nothing but a normal human situation that keeps arising again and again. Shakespeare's work has lived as long as it has because he dealt with normal human emotions — envy, ambition, rivalry, love, hate, greed, and so on. These are basic drives among us humans and are with us forever.

Because I have traveled widely it is often suspected I traveled for the purpose of gathering material. That was not the reason. Material is wherever you find it, or can *see* it. Some of the greatest novels have been written about small areas. Thomas Hardy and William Faulkner, for example, wrote about country districts they knew well. The Brontë sisters (whose name was originally Prunty) wrote about the part of England in which they lived.

It is not necessary to travel in order to write good stories; it is only necessary to see, to understand, to reveal.

What few realize is that no writer is free to write

exactly as he might wish. He is guided, to a great extent, by the tastes of readers and by the choices of editors. Of course, one can write whatever one wishes, but unless it conforms to the tastes of the public at the time, it will stay right on the author's shelf.

All manner of weird conjectures have grown up around Edgar Allan Poe, for example, but few have ever understood that he was writing what the public wanted to buy. In the first half of the nineteenth century, over in Europe, Mary Shelley was writing *Frankenstein* and Baudelaire was writing his macabre poetry and prose, while in this country, Hawthorne was writing "Rappaccini's Daughter," and Washington Irving was writing *The Legend of Sleepy Hollow.* And this has been true in every age and time.

For a while I worked in the big timber but could not bear to see the big ones come down. I topped trees for a time, cleared brush, did whatever was available, but the times were growing worse. When the crash came in '29, we who were on the road hardly noticed the difference.

Yet it was a time for decision and I had made mine. If I was ever to get an education beyond my haphazard reading, it must be now.

12

Through some boxing friends I found a job in a veneer plant in Portland, Oregon. At first I was off-bearing on a saw; later, grading veneer. We were making doors, desk tops, tables, radios, all manner of wood items, but the Depression was on and occasionally there were not enough orders to warrant a full shift.

In a second-story hotel two blocks from the library I found a room. It was a very long distance from work but close to the library and that was where I wished to be.

At the time there were two magazines, published by the same company. One was called *The Thinker*; the other, *Popular Biography*. Unfortunately, neither magazine lasted very long, perhaps because of the material, though more likely due to the Depression itself. I believe I read every issue of each, and they guided me into some areas where I might not have ventured. I carried each issue in my pocket as it came out and read them on the long bus rides to work and back.

About this time, I stumbled upon *Candide* by Voltaire, and it was a revelation. I loved it, rereading it at once. I loved the wit and the satire but above all the sense that the author himself was having a wonderful time, writing something he thoroughly enjoyed.

Shortly afterward, I went into the Reference Room of the Portland Public Library and settled down to some serious reading. From that time on, for months, I was there nearly every waking hour that the library was open and I was not working. Often I would go in at ten in the morning and not leave until ten at night. During those months I was eating only occasionally. After payday I ate rather well for a time but we were not working full shifts, and rent, transportation, and other expenses used up my money.

I had no friends at first, only acquaintances; later, working at the plant, I met a wonderful Irishman who is still a friend.

I had asked when payday was, and it was still several days away. I commented that I hoped it would come soon, because I was broke. Some time later a truck, one of those used to move stacks of lumber around inside the plant, pulled up alongside me and a tall, lean young man stepped down. He said, "They tell me you're broke until payday." He handed me $20 and said, "Pay me when you can."

That was fifty-eight years ago and that man is still my friend. We have kept in touch, off and on, all down the years.

We were working the late shift, beginning some time in midafternoon, and we got off late, so I was rarely back at the hotel before 2:00 A.M. That was, of course, when we worked a full shift.

142

One day in the library an elderly gentleman leaned over my shoulder and asked what I was reading. I had seen him around for several days, and in fact we were the only regulars in the Reference Room. Others came and went, but we were there every day. He was referring to many books, taking copious notes, and writing a lot. At the time he spoke to me I was deeply engrossed in Friedrich Schleiermacher's *Soliloquies*, and he commented that he rarely saw a young man reading philosophy.

We talked a little there, and later had coffee together. One day he brought me a manuscript which he hoped to publish. Limited as my publishing experience was, I could see he had almost no prospect of success. His paper was a brilliant piece of Socratic-type dialogue between a Citizen and a Senator, and his subject was that the Preamble to the Constitution was not intended as a Preamble but as an integral part of the Constitution.

This is the stand that Franklin Roosevelt took when he became President and which he used as authorization for some of the dramatic moves he made to turn things around. As my friend had mailed copies of his dialogue to several senators, I have often wondered if Roosevelt himself got the idea from that old gentleman in the library.

He was, like Eric Hoffer, a longshoreman.

Meanwhile I was working out in a small gym, hoping to make some money fighting. I would leave my hotel, go to the gym, get my lunch fixed at the counter in the poolroom above the gym, and go on to work.

My reading followed no pattern. I read a dozen plays by Eugene O'Neill, two by George Bernard Shaw, three by Racine, and others by Oscar Wilde, Molière, John Drinkwater, Ashley Dukes, Ferenc Molnár, and Carlo Goldoni.

In philosophy I read four books by George Santayana, three by Nietzsche, one by Schopenhauer. I read several books by H. G. Wells, at least two by Joseph Conrad, several by Rabindranath Tagore, and a real delight, *Black Sparta* by Naomi Mitchison.

Each book gave me much to think about, and on my long bus rides I frequently went over what I had read. For a while during this period I lived on one sandwich a day so I could save the money to buy three books of which I had read reviews. They were *Marriage and Morals* by Bertrand Russell, *Liberty Under the Soviets* by Roger Baldwin, and *Men and Machines* by Stuart Chase.

The subject of the influence of the machine was much under discussion at the time, as evidenced by Eugene O'Neill's play *Dynamo* and other works. Although written more than a century ago (1872), Samuel Butler's *Erewhon* is still one of the most provocative on the subject.

The paperback book, which has done so much to revolutionize reading, did not exist at the time, and hardcover books were expensive for one in my position.

Bookstores were fewer than today, when paperback books are everywhere. There were many wonderful old bookstores operated by people who both knew and loved books, and to browse their shelves was and is pure delight.

It is not uncommon today to find no one working in a bookstore who reads anything but the current best sellers, if that much. In the days I speak of, bookstores were usually operated by book lovers. Now they are run by anyone who can ring up a sale. Yet there are exceptions, and to come upon them is always a pleasure.

The work I was doing offered no chance for standing around, had I been so inclined. The plant was a noisy, busy place and we all fell into a rhythm that made the hours pass quickly, yet when the shift was over I was tired and often slept halfway back on the bus.

One night, not having bus fare, I walked back to town. I believe it was about seven miles and through a dark, deserted area along the river. Walking along, half asleep, I was suddenly startled by a man who stepped out from behind a signboard and told me to "Get 'em up."

I hit him.

It was not an intelligent reaction, nor a brave one. I was a fighter and I reacted. My punch landed solidly and he went down, the gun flying from his hand. I grabbed the gun in midair and ran at least a block before it dawned on me that I had the gun.

Whoever the man was, his tactics were bad. Had

145

he come up behind me, he could have had whatever I had, which was only a few cents, but he startled me into an instinctive reaction.

However, he was a benefactor. Back in my room I checked the pistol. It was a .38 caliber, fully loaded, but for some incomprehensible reason the barrel had never been cleared of Cosmoline or some such substance. Had he attempted to fire it he might have blown his hand off. I cleaned up the gun, took it to a pawnshop, and sold it for six dollars.

In Klamath Falls, I had worked for a time as a laborer in building the Weyerhauser Mill, working there for several months at various jobs. Each of us was expected to fill out a small slip saying what we had been doing each day. On one occasion they had me simply walking about, picking up tools, stacking spare lumber — a number of little things that needed doing — so when I filled out my slip that night, I simply wrote: "Removing obstacles in the path of progress."

The next morning the timekeeper stopped me to ask, "What the hell were you doing, anyway?"

They put a number of us to digging holes four feet square and down to hardpan for concrete piers to support a building soon to be erected. There were at least a dozen of us on the job and the ground was partly frozen. After we got down a short distance, water had to be bailed out, so progress was slow. There was a husky young German, a couple of years older than I, and we got into a contest to make the work more fun. The average was two and a half holes per day, while several were doing three. The German and I were doing four holes a day apiece.

Our boss was an easygoing Irishman who saw what was going on and wisely stayed out of it, but the management in its wisdom decided he was not gung-ho enough as a boss and brought in a new man.

Knowing nothing of any of us, he came suddenly into the area and found the German and me leaning on our shovels, having just finished our second holes for the day, while nobody else had finished one. He promptly fired both of us for loafing, along with another chap who had been doing three holes a day. In his first day on the job he had fired his three best men.

But it was time to move on, and we did.

I saw the German just once more, meeting him suddenly on the street in Portland. He was a strong, rugged guy with whom I had enjoyed wrestling around and he was also very bright. We walked the streets for hours that night, just talking of books, men, work, and the times. I have often wondered what happened to him.

That, too, was education. I learned that when I was in charge I should keep my eyes open and understand the situation before I moved. And I learned it is also risky to break up teams that are used to working together. No matter what seems to be gained, much is also lost.

Even then, I was trying to write. Often I sat alone in my room at the hotel or at a table in the library trying to tell stories. It is never so easy as it seems and I had so much to learn. If at that time I had had an income of just $100 a month of which I could be sure, it would have saved me ten years of hard work. In one year I could have learned what I needed to know, or most of it.

Writing, however, is a learning process. One never knows enough, and one is never good enough.

In so many areas my ignorance was impressive — to me, at least. One evening a girl I knew (I always knew a few here and there) read one of my efforts at verse and commented that it did not scan. I did not want to betray my ignorance, so did not ask her what she meant, but the truth was I had no idea, except that something was wrong with what I had attempted. The following day I went to the library and found a book that cleared up the mystery: *A Study of Versification* by Brander Matthews.

If one is any good as a writer at all, he must be constantly improving, learning, finding better ways of saying what needs to be said. He must also be constantly aware of what is happening in his world and in what direction it seems to be going.

My first stories were largely of the Far East, of the Indonesian waters where I had spent some time. I still have a nostalgic feeling for some of those little ports, such as Gorontalo, Amurang, and Medan. Having grown up in the West and worked around over a dozen western states, I absorbed a lot of material there and, in the years that followed, tried to absorb more.

How many nonfiction books I read about the West I do not recall, but in earlier years I had read Josiah Gregg's *Commerce of the Prairies*, which I consider one of the basic books of the westward movement. Henry Inman's book, *The Great Salt Lake Trail*, is also very good, but the West is a vast panorama and there are an infinite number of phases and aspects. The exploring, the trading and trapping, the wagon trains to Oregon and California, the Gold Rush days, the buffalo hunting, the cattle drives, the ranching, the stage-driving, the bandits, the hanging-judge period in Oklahoma and Arkansas, the sod-house settlers, the Indian-fighting in the Southwest and Northwest, the silver mining in Colorado, Utah, Nevada, and Montana, the gold mining in all those places — one could go on for a long time listing the various phases, down to the bone-pickers who gathered and sold bones left by buffalo hunters and others. Much has been written about all phases of the westward movement in this country.

One of the richest sources of understanding the westward movement is the diaries and journals of the people themselves. Reading such books or manuscripts puts the researcher on the ground at the time the events described were taking place, so one gets the *feelings* as well as the information. I have read hundreds of diaries of various lengths and have never used an incident from any of them. That is not why I read, and indeed, one rarely finds stories there. They have to be created. The material is there, the background and the situations, but one has to take this material and weave it into a story pattern.

When I do research, I am saturating myself in the time, the place, and the feelings. But reading is never enough. One must know the land. In every story of the westward movement the land itself is often the most important aspect. No one could move without knowing something of what lay ahead. What are the landmarks, if any? Where will I find water?

The journals are, as a rule, rather dull day-to-day accounts of what was happening along the way, in the town, at the ranch. These, of course, are things a writer must understand. He must see the canvas against which his story will take place.

Also, I might add, anyone who attempts to write for western readers had better know, because they do. Having a variety of cactus growing where it is never found will disgust a reader and he will toss your book aside. Western readers fire black-powder guns; they ride; they go on treks. Many of them still punch cows. Others have spent years studying various Indian tribes.

During the great days of the West, guns were changing, new rifles coming in, old ones hanging on. Some pistols were black-powder weapons loaded carefully with ball, while others were cartridge weapons. Some were converted from one to the other. Many gunfighters altered their weapons for one reason or another, and European weapons were brought in by pioneers.

To write a story of the West, one must have more accurate knowledge than for any other writing I can think of, aside from some kinds of science fiction.

One does not, as some imagine, simply "dash off a western."

A book is a friend that will do what no friend does — be silent when we wish to think.

— WILL DURANT

13

Many of the Army officers serving in the West of the period before and after the Civil War were cultured, intelligent men, and although they were defending the frontier against raids by Indians, many of them had a strong interest in the Indian and his culture. Much that we know might have been lost had it not been for their intelligent observation and comments.

On the Border with Crook by Major John G. Bourke and *Life Among the Apaches* by John C. Cremony are examples, but only two of many. That much maligned man General George Armstrong Custer — about whom more nonsense has been written by people who know nothing about him than has been written about any man in history — was another. Secretary of War William Belknap (later dismissed from office) had been appointing political friends of his as Indian agents, and they were robbing the Indians, starving them, and taking every advantage. Custer objected, but a mere Lieutenant Colonel (Custer's actual rank) got nowhere by complaining to the Secretary of War, and later they contrived an excuse for a court martial.

Custer saw the Indians being mistreated and in

his book, *My Life on the Plains*, said that if he were an Indian he would be fighting.

How many Indians were present at the Little Bighorn we will never know. Their numbers were estimated at from two thousand to nine thousand. Logic was completely on Custer's side. The Indian had never been able to field a large force because of the supply problem. When so many Indians came into an area, the game fled the country, so whatever food the Indian had he must bring with him. For the same reason he could not stay long in the field.

A fact often missed is that just a few miles south and a few days earlier, General George Crook, another of our most successful Indian fighters, had made the same mistake.

In the bitter Battle of the Rosebud, often overlooked due to the drama of the Custer massacre, Crook was fought to a standstill by many of the same Indians. Had it not been for the protests of Frank Grouard, Crook's chief of scouts, and the fact that he was down to eight rounds of ammunition per man, Crook might have pursued the Sioux down the canyon of the Rosebud into an even worse trap than Custer's, where he would have lost three times the men.

Knowing the Indian problems with supply, neither Crook on June 17 or Custer on June 25 was willing to believe that such a large force was in the field.

Few of those who write so glibly about Custer

have ever examined his career. His defeat of Jeb Stuart was without doubt one of the major reasons the North won the Battle of Gettysburg. Some may object to the term *defeat,* but without a doubt Custer prevented Stuart from obtaining his objective, and Stuart was a great cavalry officer.

Custer's troops often complained about some of his brutally long marches, but no matter how far he asked them to go, he was up there in front of them and in plain sight. The men called him old "Iron-Ass."

Often forgotten is the fact that the Seventh Cavalry, proud of its name and reputation, had an unusually large number of raw recruits when they left Fort Lincoln, which contributed to the great loss of life at the Little Bighorn.

There are so many things about Indians and their ways that were simply not known. For example: no Indian who was not present at the signing of a treaty felt bound by it. For this reason many Indians would deliberately absent themselves on such occasions.

In most cases, when a chief signed a treaty, he was signing for himself. He had no authority to force other Indians to abide by it. This most white men never understood.

In most cases the only way for a young Indian to become a man and a warrior was to take a scalp or to count coup, which meant to strike a living, armed enemy. Until he had done so, he could not get a bride and he could not speak in council. He was literally a nobody. This is why Indians often said they could not live without war.

A strike against the Indian in dealing with white men was that to him, a battle was a war. The Indian never learned about campaigns, a series of extended battles. When the Indian battle was over, all the Indians went home. The white man kept coming.

Although Crazy Horse was but one of the chiefs present at the Little Bighorn, he is usually given credit for the tactical planning. It is more likely that it grew out of a council. The fact of the matter is, had the Indians a supply system of food and ammunition, they might have whipped General Alfred Terry (Custer's commanding officer) and Gibbon as well.

That's a wild speculation, of course, but they had put Crook's command out of action and had whipped Custer and knew that Terry and Gibbon were approaching.

Personally, I do not believe that the sites of the battles were a matter of chance. I believe the Indians deliberately led the coming battle into terrain favorable to their way of fighting and where such traps as they often used were available.

Military tactics had interested me since my youth, and when I got older I read Sun-tzu, Marshal Saxe, Vegetius, Clausewitz, and dozens of others on the subject. Sun-tzu, who composed his work about 500 B.C., laid down the basic principles of military strategy and has rarely been improved upon. The American Indian used a variety of tactics but the favorite was always a variation of what

Hannibal used to defeat the Romans at Cannae. It was also used by T. E. Lawrence at the Battle of Tafila, in World War I. This was definitely what was prepared for Crook at the Rosebud but he failed to enter the trap. It also was used by the Sioux and Cheyenne at the Fetterman massacre in Wyoming, in 1866.

My mention of Vegetius, who wrote on the tactics and camps of the Roman legions, offers an opportunity to correct a mistaken impression that has long existed. When Jesus was suffering on the Cross, a Roman soldier offered him vinegar to drink, and this has been considered by many to have been an unkind act. As a matter of fact, vinegar was what the Roman legions drank, believing it a better thirst-quencher than plain water. We often put lemon in water for the same purpose. In any event, that Roman legionnaire was simply trying to share his own drink with Jesus.

Fortunately, we who write about America's frontier have no shortage of basic material. Soldiers of every rank have written of their experiences in one place or another, and the records in many areas are excellent. The only limitation on any writer is how much effort he or she is willing to put in to be accurate.

We cannot, of course, know all the story, but we do know much of it, and from what we know can easily surmise the rest. We who write fiction are not writing history, yet I do not believe anybody has a right to alter history for the sake of a story. If nothing else, it betrays a lack of creative ability. The actual history is amazing enough and I prefer to put my characters into what is actually happening and let it happen to them.

My reading in the library continued with *Why We Behave Like Human Beings* by George A. Dorsey, *Thus Spake Zarathustra* and *The Will to Power* by Nietzsche, a volume of essays by Schopenhauer, and another by William James.

In fiction I read *The Case of Sergeant Grischa* by Arnold Zweig, which I consider the best novel to come out of World War I, although Remarque's *All Quiet on the Western Front* attracted more attention and was a good book also. I read *The Master Mind of Mars* by Edgar Rice Burroughs, a continuation of the series I had read when I was twelve. *Bitter Bierce* by C. Hartley Grattan was a biography of one of my long-time favorites, Ambrose Bierce.

Becoming briefly interested in psychiatry, I read two books by Coriat, as well as the *Psychology of Insanity* by Bernard Hart, and *The Mind at Mischief* by William Sadler.

In the meanwhile, my brother Parker and I had been developing a small conspiracy. My parents were living in Oregon at the time, near Klamath Falls. I was preparing to move on from Portland. When I did, they would be some distance from any of the family, and they were growing older.

Parker was Washington correspondent for the *Oklahoman-Times*, dividing his time between Oklahoma City and Washington, D.C. So we planned to find an excuse to get my parents to move to Oklahoma. Parker bought an acreage east of Oklahoma City near Choctaw and began telling Dad the difficulties he was having in getting anyone to plant trees, care for them, and generally protect the place.

The upshot of it was that Dad decided to drive down and see what he could do, and I was to make the trip with them.

We could not know then that Parker was soon to leave for a job with Scripps-Howard in Ohio, and would only occasionally visit in Oklahoma.

Using a name I had never used before and never used again, I entered an amateur boxing contest and fought but one fight, which I lost. Most of my fighting was done in small-town rings, with only here and there a venture into big city clubs. I never did well in the amateurs, largely because I was not eating as regularly as I should and because of conditions generally. As I had the idea I might someday turn to boxing seriously I did not want a blemish on what I hoped would be a good record.

I was working nights, dead tired, and they tied the gloves on us well before we were to enter the ring, as is often done in amateur bouts where many end quickly. I was so tired I fell asleep waiting to be called to the ring.

I fought a fairly good fight, with one flurry in the second round that won the round for me, but lost the decision to a good fighter.

In all I read 115 books and plays in 1930.

I do not believe that any writer has ever presented an account of his reading or education. Some of what I am writing here may seem dull stuff, but I have enjoyed digging into the reading habits of many great men and women and have tried where possible to get a list of the books in their libraries. I have in mind a book about the American Revolution which I am eager to write, though unhappily the time may not be allowed me, as I have so many projects on the fire and could not do them all in two lifetimes. However, in researching this book, I had occasion to visit the estate of George Mason and there I collected a list of the books he had in his study and those he had read in preparing himself. He was without a doubt one of the most influential men of his time, and the sources of his ideas were important to me. Still, a book is less important for what it says than for what it makes you think.

I hoped that by understanding the books these men and women read I might grasp at the basic sources of some of their ideas.

In several of my western novels I have had characters reading Plutarch. I believe more great men have read his *Lives* than any other book, except possibly the Bible. But, as many pagans read Plutarch, his work may still be the most widely read. In reviewing the reading histories or libraries of great men, I have come upon him again and again, and justly so. His is a sophisticated, urbane mind dealing with aspects of leadership.

Once more now, I was upon the road, this time with my parents, traveling through eastern Oregon, a section of Idaho, into Wyoming, and on to Oklahoma. Each night in some café or other stopping place I sought out the people who knew about the area. It was always easy to get them started, and all that remained was to listen.

In each town there are collections of pamphlets about local history, but once you leave the town they are rarely available elsewhere. I had it in mind to build a library and gather them all together, from every state in the union, as a source for scholarly research.

I know that I have profited much from such accounts — often simply some old pioneer or soldier telling how it was. Many of these booklets are only a few pages, but each has value in itself. Our land is rich beyond belief in the memories of its pioneers but much of this material is being lost through sheer lack of awareness that it exists. Many of the best stories of our country are in such booklets, unavailable to scholars, and many of them can throw revealing light on the pages of history.

In talking with old-timers I learned very quickly that they read books, too, or heard stories from others who had. As I had read everything they were likely to know, I could recognize the stories as they appeared. I just let them talk, telling stories about Billy the Kid, Wild Bill Hickok (his ancestors were once tenant farmers for William

Shakespeare), or the O.K. Corral. I had taken the precaution of learning the names of a couple of local characters, perhaps an old-time cowboy, a rancher, miner or whatever. After letting the old-timer have his period of talking of things of which he thought only he knew, I would bring up the local character and immediately be treated to a flood of stories and memories. Others listening would chime in with their viewpoints. When that happens, you get the real stories, not watered-down versions of what somebody believed happened.

Nowadays, when traveling in the West, I am often told about old-timers — who usually turn out to be younger than I am — who have stories to tell. Occasionally they are stories repeated from ones their fathers or mothers told, but too often they are partially digested, often-told stories that have been well written long before.

There are so many wonderful stories to be written, and so much material to be used. When I hear people talking of writer's block, I am amazed.

Start writing, no matter about what. The water does not flow until the faucet is turned on. You can sit and look at a page for a long time and nothing will happen. Start writing and it will.

14

Our trip to Oklahoma was taken at a leisurely pace. There was no reason for hurry, and we all liked to see the country. Occasionally we turned off the highway to visit an old fort or a ranch. At night I was reading Theodor Mommsen's *History of Rome*, and Livy as well. Dipping into one and then the other, I found myself wishing I had Polybius. In the past I had read from him, and liked him better, I believe, than Livy.

I was by no means a scholar, simply an interested reader with nothing to do but live and learn, traveling through what a few years earlier had been Indian country. Driving beside trails still rutted by wagon trains, I was getting history from two aspects: that of ancient times and those just past. It was a means of putting things in perspective.

Each people is, I believe, inclined to believe it is the purpose of history, that all that has happened is leading to now, to this world, this country. Few of us see ourselves as fleeting phantoms on a much wider screen, or that our great cities may someday be dug from the ruins by archeologists of the future.

Surely, the citizens and the rulers of Babylon and Rome did not see themselves as a passing phase. Each in its time believed it was the end-all of the world's progression. I have no such feeling. Each age is a day that is dying, each one a dream that is fading.

Someday, men — or some other intelligent creatures — will stand on the sites of New York or Los Angeles and wonder if anyone ever lived there.

We know so little of the past, and what we have discovered is largely what lies above water. Yet once, sea level was lower, and no doubt there are cities of which we know nothing that once existed there. If something were to happen now, nothing might remain of our world but the faces on Mount Rushmore or the figures on Stone Mountain, and perhaps the foundations of some of our freeways.

Of the hundreds of plays written by Euripides, Aristophanes, Sophocles, and others, we have but a few. At least two hundred plays, whose titles we know, have vanished, and if so many plays, how many books on history, medicine, or other subjects, with probably fewer copies released at the time, are missing?

I have delved deeply into the literatures of the world, yet what is available is scarcely a dusting of what must have been. Great libraries have been destroyed, and books or manuscripts are vulnerable.

Books as books must be preserved. There is an effort now to preserve everything by mechanical means, but of what use will they be to a man who has no power? No means of reproducing the sounds or the words? A book can be carried away and read at leisure. It needs nothing but an eye, a brain, and the ability to read.

If in some distant future, someone should come upon the remains of a library of ours, even if he could not read, he could through illustrations rediscover much otherwise lost. He would have no machine with which to play a tape; he would have no source of power.

In my library of some ten thousand selected books, I have the means of reproducing much of our civilization. I have the five volumes of Singer's *History of Technology*, which have much on the means of construction. There are other books on the building of watercraft, books on all manner of crafts and how they were done. From there alone, if all were lost, one might start again.

Of the value of books I am myself my best example. If it were not for books, I should never have been more than a laborer, perhaps killed in a mine disaster, as some of my friends were. Yet the books were there, I could read, and had the will to read and the persistence to keep on reading. To date I have lectured in more than forty colleges and universities, and enjoyed every minute of it. I have been able in some small way to contribute to the entertainment and perhaps the knowledge of the world.

Actors, politicians, and writers — all of us are but creatures of the hour. Long-lasting fame comes to but few. Turning the pages of my notebooks,

I see so many names, once well known, now all but forgotten.

I am thinking of Count Hermann Keyserling, who wrote among other things *The Travel Diary of a Philosopher*. I have not heard his name mentioned in years, yet he wrote well and entertainingly. Another is one who considered himself the glamour boy of his time. I refer to Gabriele D'Annunzio, who wrote *The Flame of Life* but is probably best remembered as a lover of Eleanora Duse.

Speaking of her, I shall repeat a story no doubt most have heard, but I love it. Sarah Bernhardt, another great actress of her time, finally got a chance to see Duse on the stage and, overcome with the greatness of the performance, wrote a very quick note to send backstage. It said: "Sarah Bernhardt says Eleanora Duse is a great actress." Busy changing costume for the next act, Eleanora Duse had no time to compose a reply, so she picked up a pen and added two commas to the note and returned it. Now it read: "Sarah Bernhardt, says Eleanora Duse, is a great actress."

We stopped one night at a ranch where the people were known to me. Originally, I had come to the place riding the grub-line with a cowboy who used to work on the ranch. We had stayed, told stories, and generally enjoyed ourselves, so I thought we would stop by and say hello. My father, who was a veterinarian, took time out to fix the teeth on a couple of horses at the ranch, and in the evening, as we sat on the porch, I happened to comment that an uncle of mine by marriage had known Butch Cassidy.

The rancher commented that Butch had been through not long before, driving a Dodge, and had swapped a couple of tires for a saddle.

Butch was supposed to have been killed in South America but a lot of people in Utah and Wyoming knew better.

Butch had always been a cheerful, friendly man and nobody was ever killed in a holdup in this country in which he was involved. Having been a working cowboy himself, he understood his people. Most cowboys and many others would cheerfully join a posse for the fun of it, and would pursue an outlaw not too closely, but if that outlaw had killed a man with a family, it was a different story, and it was no longer a chase for fun. Yet even the officers who pursued Butch liked him personally. If he had enemies other than the Pinkertons, I have never heard of them.

After the others had gone to bed, I sat up by a coal-oil lamp reading of the decline of Hannibal's fortunes, from his great victory at Cannae to his defeat at Zama. At the critical time when Hannibal might have destroyed the power of Rome, the peace party in Carthage refused support, and he was eventually defeated and Carthage destroyed.

When I finished the chapter I was reading, I remember walking out on the porch and sitting there in the darkness, listening to the coyotes talking to the moon. It was dark and still, the voices of the coyotes seeming to emphasize the silence. I remember sitting there for a long time, thinking of what I had read and of the many wagons that had passed this way bound for California and Oregon.

Livy, I had read before, and a bit of Mommsen, but I had only dipped into Tacitus. I was not to read him until, during World War II, a lovely young lady sent me, at my request, a copy of the Modern Library edition. Gibbon's *Decline and Fall* I had read in pieces here and there but never the entire work, but I would soon. Rome was interesting to me not only for its own exciting history but because of its great contributions to law, organization, and the civilizing of Europe. Even during the dark days of Nero and Caligula, the Roman Empire was governed well. The terrors they brought were largely spent on their associates at court; the administration in the provinces was only slightly affected, if at all.

Further along on that trip I read a volume of poetry by Swinburne, *Castle Gay* by John Buchan, and *The Prince* by Machiavelli. My father was driving, and often when we'd be passing through a wide-open area where there was not much new to see, I would read while riding. Many times I read aloud, as I was to do later when traveling with my children. We always had a book going.

Behind me lay many cities, many seaport towns, many men of all kinds whom I had met and known. Reading the *Odyssey* by Homer, I often thought how like some of his characters were men whom

I had met. As I have said elsewhere, there is a kinship between men who have lived in the dynamic periods of history, and Achilles or Ajax would have been perfectly at home at the Alamo or the Battle of Adobe Walls, and Davy Crockett or Jim Bowie could have walked a quarter-deck beside Ulysses or Sir Francis Drake. All were men of action and of driving ambition and would have understood one another with no problem.

We arrived at last at a small white house in Oklahoma, seated on ten acres of land that soon became twenty, part of it in blackjack (a kind of scrub oak) and badly scarred by erosion.

My intention was to see my parents settled and then go on to New Orleans and the sea. It was still in my mind to work for a Third Mate's ticket and stay at sea until I had written a book or two.

It was not to be. I had no way of knowing I had reached a destination, and when I left there at last, all was changed and my life was well set on the course it was to follow until now.

We unpacked and walked out to look at the land. In the worst of the eroded gullies, we packed some old barbed wire and some dead branches to catch and hold debris during the rains, built a few small dams, and started planting trees — mostly plum trees, as I recall.

We had two horses on the place and one of them took to following me like a puppy, especially when I was rabbit hunting. Killing rabbits was almost the price of survival if one wished to raise a garden, either of vegetables or of flowers. I had a .22 rifle and had always been a good shot. I preferred using a pistol but I noticed that our neighbors looked on me with some suspicion when I wore the pistol, but not when I carried the rifle. My small war against the rabbits was as much for the neighbors as for ourselves. It was a war I never won, but I did reduce the odds.

The Great Depression was in full swing and there was no market for produce. People were living on what they could raise, and although many were good farmers, their crops often rotted in the fields. Several times I went away, to fight in various towns or to make a brief trip to sea, always returning, for I had settled down to become a writer.

For years I had written, publishing a bit of poetry for no pay, contributing an article or two to newspapers, writing a few boxing stories (like the one in Klamath Falls, written for two girl reporters who had never seen a fight). I had always been able to put words together in a readable fashion. I did not know what a story was, although, like everybody else, I believed I did.

My brother had been sent an advance copy of *Anthony Adverse* by Hervey Allen, and I wrote a review of it and sent it to the *Sunday Oklahoman*. As I mentioned earlier, the book editor was Kenneth C. Kaufman, a professor of romance languages at the University of Oklahoma. He was also one of the editors of *Books Abroad*, an international quarterly that reviewed books in several languages. Kaufman published the review, in which I predicted the success of *Anthony Adverse,* and later sent me two more books for review, one of which was *The Memoirs of Vincent Nolte,* a real character who was Anthony's good friend in the novel. It has proved to be a very valuable source book for me, also.

In the meanwhile I had read a number of plays by Ibsen, Shaw, Molnar, and Robert E. Sherwood, as well as the novels *The Magic Mountain* by Thomas Mann, *Penguin Island* by Anatole France, *The Red and the Black* by Stendhal, *Wuthering Heights* by Emily Brontë, and a half-dozen books by Gustave Flaubert, including *Madame Bovary.* Slowly, I was learning what had been written and how writers approached their various subjects, while always I was trying to get my own work published, first with poetry, then with articles and stories. But they got nowhere at all.

There was a steady flow of rejection slips. Once in a while, a handwritten word, *Sorry,* appeared on the slip. I was grateful for even that bit of attention.

My secret was that no sooner did I put something in the mail than I wrote something else and sent it off. Each rejection was cushioned by my expectations for the other manuscripts. Too many writers put their all into one script, and when it is rejected they are devastated.

Having no rhyming dictionary, I made one myself in a small notebook, on the back pages, while on the reverse side I listed my submissions and their fate. The notebook shows page after page of rejections with, after a while, an occasional acceptance from one of the little magazines that did not pay for material. There were then, as now, a number of such ventures, some of them published at universities, some by daring individuals with little capital and much hope.

Often the magazines faded into the sunset before they got beyond the wishful stages, and my work faded with them — which, as I remember some of it, was just as well.

In the meanwhile I continued my defensive war against the rabbits, faithfully followed by our horse, who would hang his head over my shoulder and, when I fired, would run forward, smell the dead rabbit, toss his head and roll his eyes, but follow me eagerly when I went out again.

Thoughts are like flowers; those gathered in the morning keep fresh the longest.

— ANDRÉ GIDE

15

Much of the first poetry I wrote was composed while walking in the evening, looking for rabbits but not really hunting. If a rabbit was so unfortunate as to come my way, that was one thing, but I was not looking. The evenings were quiet, twilight lasted, and it was pleasant walking along the country road (at that time unpaved).

About a quarter of a mile from our house, perhaps a bit more, there was a larger house setting not far from the main road. On this evening as I came along, a farmer was picketing a calf on the grass in front of the house. I greeted him and stopped to pass the time of day. Noticing a book in my pocket, he asked what it was.

Earlier, I had been reading Charles Baudelaire's *Poems and Prose* in a limp cloth edition and when I started on my walk simply thrust it in my back pocket. That led us to a discussion of books and reading, and I found the man, whose name was Gillespie, a very erudite gentleman with a face that reminded me of pictures of Ralph Waldo Emerson.

If I remember correctly I believe he told me he had been one of the editors of the Kansas Socialist newspaper, *The Appeal to Reason*. At least there had been some connection. As he grew older he had moved a little more to the right side of the political spectrum, but not much.

He invited me in, and we sat down in the living room of the old house. I looked around. Obviously he was a bachelor and not too concerned with housekeeping. A couple of old coats hung from a hook on the wall, some crinkled boots lay on their sides, but there was a good table, a fine lamp, and several bookshelves overcrowded with books, as mine always are.

He had Karl Marx's *Capital*, Adam Smith's *Wealth of Nations*, a volume by the English economist David Ricardo (the title of which escapes me), along with much poetry and history.

During subsequent months we were to have many long conversations on books, writers, history, and all subjects pertaining to any of them. He was a gentle, thoughtful man, a pipe smoker and a good farmer who gave most of his produce away.

On that first visit I borrowed from him *History of the Intellectual Development of Europe* in two volumes by John W. Draper, a very good history that deserves more attention than it ever received. It was in his home, too, that I first encountered the Introduction to *The History of Civilization in England* by Henry Buckle, and later borrowed and read the first volume of a two-volume *The Decline and Fall of the Roman Empire*, by Gibbon.

About that time I read *Harlem Shadows* by Claude McKay, one of several very good black poets being published then.

I also read books by Lion Feuchtwanger, D. H. Lawrence, Maxim Gorky, Nietzsche, Whitehead, and Freud, by Molière, France, Turgenev, Victor Hugo, Wilde, Poe, Thoreau, Emerson, George Eliot, and Goethe.

Aside from Gillespie, we had no close friends among our neighbors. We knew a few of them but there was no visiting. From time to time, I heard rumors that many thought I should be out rustling for a job instead of staying at home. Every day I put in hours at the typewriter but, aside from Gillespie, these were not people to take that seriously.

There were in the nearby town several young men who devoted their time to sitting along the curb and drinking an occasional beer. They did not know me except that I came to town, mailed manuscripts, and drank coffee. A druggist from whom I bought magazines warned me once that I should be careful.

The warning was not needed, for I had been a stranger in too many towns not to read their faces, but I had also sized them up pretty well. They were loafers and talkers, soft around the middle, probably knowing little enough about fighting, and I was not worried. Aside from the boxing I had done, I had served my time in mining and lumber-camp fights and in some brutal waterfront fighting, where utter savagery is the rule, so I was not disturbed.

Having lived and worked here and overseas, I

knew they were not equipped for the kind of fighting I understood. (Karate and kung fu, incidentally, were relatively unknown in this country before World War II and the Korean War. At that time many G.I.'s learned something of the martial arts and brought them home.) Those of us who had lived along the waterfronts of Shanghai, Hong Kong, Taku Bar, Singapore, and other such places had picked up a bit here and there. None of us would have qualified for a black belt, although two brothers who gave me instruction at one time were masters, not only of the above martial arts but of several others no longer taught. Unfortunately many of the Oriental masters kept their secrets to themselves or for special students, and if one died, his knowledge might be lost forever.

Fighting four men may not be as tough as beating one really good fighter. Two will usually hang back, to come in at the finish when they will not get hurt, and the thing to do is destroy the first man who attacks or whom you presume to be the toughest aggressor. If one tough man goes down, all the steam can go out of an attack. Of course, this is not always the case. In any event, I was not worried.

There came a day when I walked the three miles into town to mail a manuscript and while there discovered there was to be a baseball game at the high school. The quality of baseball played by the teams in that area had developed several major league players of real ability, so I decided to walk back and see the game.

As the game was winding down, three young local men came over to me and said they had heard I was a boxer. How would I like to put on the gloves with a local fighter?

It was the last thing I wanted. Already I had walked nine miles, had been on my feet a good bit of the time during the ball game, and was tired. Yet this was a chance to avoid future trouble.

So I agreed, and was introduced to a rugged youngster who looked good. As we started toward the gym, I said, "Are we going to kill each other or just give them a nice boxing match?"

He said, "I wasn't looking for this. They conned me into it."

From the moment I saw him, I liked him. I had thought of going out and really doing a job on whomever I was asked to face, but once I saw him I changed my mind. This was a good kid, not one of the rowdy crowd.

We put on the gloves and boxed three light, fast rounds. He moved well, was tough, and he could punch. He also had a very bad habit of knocking down a left-hand lead with his left hand, exposing his jaw to a right.

It was a nice bout and I enjoyed it. More than that, I liked him, and he had what it took to make a fighter. After we took off the gloves I heard no more about anybody laying for me on my way home, but as we parted I suggested we should get together, that I would like to train him.

In the next few months I developed a Golden

Gloves boxing team of four to eight boys, and three of them, including the above fighter, won novice championships in their divisions. The boy I had boxed first had to share his title with his brother, rather than face him in the ring. They had cleaned up all the opposition.

Often I am asked if any writer ever helped or advised me. None did. However, I was not asking for help either, and I do not believe one should. If one wishes to write, he or she had better be writing, and there is no real way in which one writer can help another. Each must find his own way, as I was to find mine.

My way may not be for anyone but me. In fact, I doubt it is. After many rejections I sat down on the porch one night where I worked, looked off through our growing plum trees, and decided that all the editors who rejected my work could not be mistaken. Something was basically wrong with what I was doing.

From my shelves I took several stories by O. Henry, Guy de Maupassant, Jack London, and Conan Doyle. From popular magazines I took several that I had liked, and I settled down to study them, to see what those writers were doing that I was not. Later, I added stories by Maxim Gorky and Robert Louis Stevenson.

About that time I received a note from Professor Kaufman suggesting that I visit him at the University. It was on that occasion that he introduced me to a number of his friends and when I met

Professor Walter Campbell, who also wrote as Stanley Vestal. (Sometime later he, in conjunction with a former pulp-fiction writer, Foster Harris, started a short course in professional writing, where I was to appear eight or nine times as a lecturer on writing the short story.)

Campbell had published a number of books on a variety of subjects, but most were connected with the opening of the West. He had written or was writing a biography of Sitting Bull, and as I had grown up in Dakota, where the Custer story was still on everybody's lips when I was a child, we talked about it occasionally.

Although no one in Professor Kaufman's group was making a living by writing, all had published books and written a good bit for the journals. Most of them also reviewed books for the same page on which my book reviews appeared. They were a friendly, easygoing crowd and I made some good friends among them.

Above all, they were writers, the first I had actually met.

Shortly after my visit, I placed my first story for publication. It was a hobo story, submitted to a magazine that had published many famous names when they were starting out. The magazine paid on publication, but that never happened. The magazine folded after accepting my story and that was the end of it.

Meanwhile I had published some poetry in small journals, one of them published at Emory University, where former President Jimmy Carter now teaches. This sonnet was to appear later in my book of verse, *Smoke from This Altar.*

That book, incidentally, was dedicated "To Singapore Charlie, Who Couldn't Read." So he would never know. Charlie would have done well in Hollywood or as a professional wrestler. On second thought, not as a wrestler. He took his fighting seriously.

I met him first at the Straits Hotel, not the one by that name now, but one that existed before. He was about five feet nine and weighed 250 pounds. Without doubt, he had the largest bones and was the strongest man I ever knew.

When we met he was working as Bo'sun on a trading schooner in the East Indies and doubling as engineer in handling the auxiliary engine on the schooner. He was a man of no education, but was a skilled engineer and mechanic as well as a fine seaman.

His father had been a Portuguese Negro who married, I believe, a girl of mixed Chinese and Malay ancestry. Around each wrist and ankle Charlie had a rope tattooed, and everything in between was covered by some stylish artistry, the best the tattoo parlors of the Far East could offer — which was very good, indeed. My favorite bit, however, was on his neck. Around it was tattooed a dotted line and the words *Cut on the dotted line.*

We worked together for a while and Charlie was awed by the fact that I was forever with a book.

He could not read, as I have said, but somehow he had great respect for anyone who did. From time to time, circumstances demanded I go into some very tough places, and I always took Charlie with me. Beyond everything else, the man had presence. When he walked into a tough waterfront bar, the crowd just opened before him.

As a younger man he had been a noted bolo fighter — an event where disputes are settled by tying the fighters' left wrists together while each of them takes a bolo knife in the right hand. After the first few fights Charlie found no takers; his strength was simply too great.

He disappeared somewhere during the war in the South Pacific, but I am sure he did not go gently into that good night.

In 1935, I sold my first short story for cash — a very small bit of cash indeed, for a short-short called "Anything for a Pal." It was a gangster story, published in *True Gang Life*, and I was paid $6.54.

My next story was bought by Leo Margulies, whom any pulp writer of the time will remember. Leo was to buy many stories from me in the years that followed and to become a good friend. For a writer he was an angel in disguise, for in those rough years when I was living check to check, Leo always paid quickly. I could send him a story and know I would have a check within two weeks, often sooner.

My first stories were not of the West, but of

the Far East or of the prize ring. My toe was in the door I had so long wanted to see open before me, but as for my education, it was only beginning.

When I wrote my first western story I do not remember, but I was writing many stories on many subjects. The West was where I had grown up. I knew the people, the land, and the work they did. It was an easy step for me to write about the West.

I am probably the last writer who will ever have known the people who lived the frontier life. In drifting about across the West, I have known five men and two women who knew Billy the Kid, two who rode in the Tonto Basin war in Arizona, and a variety of others who were outlaws, or frontier marshals like Jeff Milton, Bill Tilghman, and Chris Madsen, or just pioneers. I hear from some of their relatives from time to time, and it is always a pleasure.

Although I saw Bill Tilghman on only two occasions, I knew his widow quite well. Zoe Tilghman was herself a writer and we appeared on programs together.

My reading continued — Francis Bacon, Plato, Tolstoy, Immanuel Kant, Herbert Spencer, and a dozen plays by Shakespeare, whom I had read intermittently over the years. He was the ultimate professional, a writer who knew what he was doing all the time.

I also read the work of a black poet who wrote

in dialect and so, I suspect, is frowned upon today, but not by me. Paul Laurence Dunbar was a good poet with a grand sense of humor. I liked his poetry then and I like it now.

16

There is a tendency, I believe, sometimes to judge the life-style of a whole people by what we know of a group. Writers and artists are inclined to life-styles different from those of artisans or farmers, merchants or soldiers.

Most of what history we have was written by people who did not labor for their bread, or if they did, like Socrates, they often courted or associated with a different kind of people from their fellow workmen. We know all too little of how work was done in times past, as such things were deemed beneath notice, a matter for slaves or other laborers. Most of our pictures of ancient life are offered us by an elite group, concerned with themselves and their way of life.

Here and there we have been fortunate enough, as in the case of the Egyptians, to have some illustration of how things were done, but histories such as we have from ancient times deal largely with wars, kings, and orations. Occasionally there is a book such as *The Journal of My Life* by Jacques-Louis Menetra — a glazier of the time prior to and during the French Revolution — which provides a picture of how a working man lived, worked, and played. Such books are all too rare.

If we had only Greenwich Village as an example, it would tell us nothing of the rest of America, yet often one discovers a writer, or several of them, giving just such a narrow picture. One should tread warily when using the life-style of any group as an example of the thinking or the practice of a people.

Beginning in 1931, I read all of George Bernard Shaw that was available, including his novel about the bare-knuckle fighting days, *Cashel Byron's Profession.* Shaw knew a surprising lot about boxing, understanding among other things that a taped and bandaged fist inside a glove strikes with much greater force than a bare fist. There never was such a thing as a punch-drunk fighter until the boxing glove was invented, and increasing the size of the gloves has not protected the fighter more, only made boxing less scientific, as it now takes a larger opening for a punch to get through.

Shaw's knowledge of boxing was not surprising in an Irishman, though it was surprising in one whom James Huneker described as "a wingless angel with an old maid's temperament."

Shaw was a many-sided man, not easily understood — and not wishing to be understood — as a person. At least, such is my impression. He left school at the age of fourteen and educated himself, eventually becoming a music and drama critic in London. His novels, and he wrote half a dozen, were not successful. In later years he said he remembered them only as five brown paper packages that kept coming back marked *Postage Due.*

Writing as a craft varies much from individual to individual. Probably no two writers write in the same way in any respect. Some write very slowly, like Gustave Flaubert, who needed seven years to complete *Madame Bovary.* On the other hand, William Shakespeare, Honoré de Balzac, Charles Dickens, and Anthony Trollope (to name a few) wrote with considerable speed. Some writers are prolific; some are not. It has nothing to do with the quality of their work; the speed or frequency of their writing is a matter of personal inclination or temperament.

Shakespeare, who was a working actor during most of his life, and during all his writing years, wrote swiftly, completing in most years two plays while appearing in others. In his time it was the customary thing for his company to offer two plays each week, one old and one new, and the latter undoubtedly required some rehearsal or at least a run-through. His writing was done backstage, in taverns, in the homes of friends, or in his own quarters. As he was usually assisting in the management of the company and later of the theater, his time was well filled.

Writing is not an easy profession and many go reluctantly to the desk. This has never been a problem for me. I have found many stories to tell, although my first novel was never completed due to the coming of World War II. It lies on a shelf now, but would need considerable work.

People are always interested in how a writer works, as if that made a difference. Some imagine a writer must have complete quiet, or some special atmosphere. The fact is, a professional writer can write anywhere, although some environments are undoubtedly more favorable than others. Some excellent writing is done these days by newspaper people working in a bustling, busy newsroom.

Personally, I prefer my study or my bedroom at the ranch. In the first place, I am surrounded by my library, where I can check any fact that requires it. At the ranch I have a view of the timbered mountain ridge at the back of my property, or I can look up a valley in the hills where the elk and deer come down to feed in the evening. Forty or fifty can be there at once, as we do not allow hunting, and they are beautiful to watch.

However, I began my writing in ship's fo'c'sles, bunkhouses, hotel rooms — wherever I could sit down with a pen and something to write on.

Because we know so little of how people worked, we often do not know if they had machines beyond the simplest of water wheels, wagons, and such. But recently an astrolabe was found in an ancient ship, and that intrigues me. Here was a scientific instrument, a sort of computer, if you will, built of gears similar to the inner workings of a watch. Certainly this was not one of a kind, and the same principles, gears, and such must have been used for other things. One such machine does

Louis at three years old.

My home [in Jamestown, North Dakota], *where I was born.*

Twelve years old.

My father, Dr. L.C. La Moore (he altered the spelling).

Luflander [a fellow seaman from S.S. *Steelworker*], *Malay barber, myself at eighteen, Balikpapan, Borneo.*

The **Steadfast,** *one of the ships I went to sea on.*

(From right to left) Friends Bill Morrissey,
Rich Morrissey, Evan Lougheed, Art Ringuette,
and Louis L'Amour, about 1922–23.
(Photo courtesy of Irene S. Westley.)

Katherine Bunk House [Katherine Mine,
Kingman, Arizona], *Dad and myself. Eighteen
years old. Just returned from around the world on
a freighter, the* Steelworker.

*Yoba Copper Company, where I was caretaker of
a mine for three months.*

*Choctaw, Oklahoma. Oak and myself shortly after
we arrived from Oregon.*

I was a Lieutenant in this outfit [the 3622 Transportation Corps.].

(From left to right) Dingman, another man from my outfit, the Countess Guitou de Felcourt (with her two children, Bruno and Thérèse) and me on the steps of the Chateau Andrezel where the countess lived.

At the typewriter, Los Angeles apartment, 1953.

In Central Park, New York City, 1954.

On the set of *Guns of the Timberland*, 1959, with Alan Ladd. The inscription reads: "To Louis — Write another one — I'm with you — Alan, '59". Alan's own company produced the film.

Louis and Kathy L'Amour near the location where *Heller with a Gun* was being filmed as *Heller in Pink Tights* (c. 1959–1960).

With son Beau, 1964.

With daughter Angelique, c. 1969.

In Colorado, mid-1970's.

Louis and Kathy L'Amour near the old Roman theater in Arles, France, 1985. (Photo by Susan Williams.)

In Batz-sur-Mer, France, in the spring of 1985, in the footsteps of *The Walking Drum's* Kerbouchard. (Photo by Susan Williams.)

not come from nothing. But how many other such machines or instruments might have been in use at the time?

If our civilization should be destroyed now, or should simply die, in five hundred to a thousand years nothing would remain but a few stone carvings. All of our vaunted machine civilization would have rusted or eroded away and nothing would be left to indicate what we had been and what we had done. Gold alone lasts; silver disappears, as was discovered in the ruins of Ur of the Chaldees.

I continued my reading: *The History of the Conquest of Mexico* and *The History of the Conquest of Peru* by William Prescott, *The French Revolution* by Thomas Carlyle, *A Sentimental Journey* by Laurence Sterne, *To Have and Have Not* by Ernest Hemingway, a good bit of John Dos Passos, *Union Square* and *The Foundry* by Albert Halper, and that utterly delightful book by Leonard Q. Ross (Leo Rosten), *The Education of H*Y*M*A*N K*A*P*L*A*N*. By this point I had also read *The History of English Literature*, in four volumes, by Taine, and particularly enjoyed his comments on Shakespeare and his picture of the English theater of the time.

Meanwhile I also continued to review books, including *The Story of Dictatorship* by E. E. Kellett, *The 101 Ranch* by Ellsworth Collings, *Discovery* by Admiral Byrd, and *Letters from Iceland* by W. H. Auden and Louis MacNeice. In that one

193

year I reviewed twenty-two books.

Maxwell Anderson I had read at intervals until I completed everything of his I could find. He had gone to high school in my hometown, where his father was an itinerant minister, and he had been on a debating team with my sister Edna. Edna and his sister corresponded for many years. He was gone from Jamestown before I knew it, so I never met him, although I enjoyed much of his work.

At the time I settled down in Oklahoma to become a writer or else, the short story was the thing. There were many magazines publishing short stories, and many people reading them. To a writer the magazine field was divided into three categories. The so-called quality publications included *Harper's*, *The Atlantic Monthly*, *The American Mercury* (edited by H. L. Mencken), *Esquire*, *The New Yorker* (to which I was a very early subscriber while working at the Katherine Mine in Arizona), and *Story*.

The latter publication had begun as a mimeographed sheet published in Vienna, where Whit Burnett and Martha Foley lived at the time. It became the bible of the short story, publishing early work by William Saroyan, among others. Its pages were literally "who was who" in the writing field. If memory serves me right, the magazine published stories by five Nobel Prize winners in one year.

However, they paid very little, and the number

of people who could write quality stories for the above magazines far exceeded the market.

Next in line for a working writer were the "slicks," a number of popular magazines published on smooth paper, which included *The Saturday Evening Post, Ladies' Home Journal,* and *Collier's.* For a time, *Liberty, Cosmopolitan,* and *Redbook* also fell into that group. There were a half-dozen others of equal or lesser standing. This was the best-paying market.

The Saturday Evening Post and *Collier's* were weekly publications, used a lot of material, and paid excellent prices, but selling to them was not easy. They had a number of regulars whose stories were popular with *Post* readers. One of these was Clarence Budington Kelland. During the course of a year the *Post* usually published several western serials, and western short stories often appeared there by writers such as James Warner Bellah and Ernest Haycox, for example, and somewhat later, Luke Short.

Considerably later, a serial of mine called *The Burning Hills* appeared there (in five installments), as did several of my short stories.

The third category of magazines were the pulps, so-called because they were printed on wood-pulp paper. There were many of them, dozens of western and mystery magazines, others publishing science fiction, sports stories, romance, war, and air stories. Two of the best were *Adventure* and *Blue Book. Black Mask,* one of the mystery magazines, was a breeding ground for such writers as Dashiell

Hammett, Raymond Chandler, and Cornell Woolrich, who also wrote as William Irish and was distinctly one of the best.

This was the magazine market I faced as a beginning writer. There were many other magazines that bought articles or occasional fiction, and many of the writers for the quality publications were academics teaching at various colleges or employed elsewhere.

For me there was no choice. Whatever else I did, I had to make a living from my writing, and that meant work and lots of it.

Fortunately I had a wide range of experience and was able to move in more than one direction. And what I did not know, I could find out.

Gustave Flaubert said once that "Talent is nothing but long patience."

No doubt that is at least partly true. Certainly, in the years when I was beginning as a writer, I met a number of young men and women with similar ambitions. Often they wrote things so brilliant that I envied them their facility with words and ideas, yet of the dozen or so I knew then, only one made it as a professional, and he became Sunday editor of a newspaper. The others all fell by the wayside, unable or unwilling to take rejection, and obviously incapable of that long patience of which Flaubert speaks.

It was necessary that I sell stories, and to sell them they had to be written, so I wrote. No sooner was a story in the mail than I wrote another, and another. I like to tell stories. I have always enjoyed it, yet writing is always and forever a learning process. One is never good enough and one never knows enough. I cannot repeat that too often. No matter how good a writer becomes, he can always be better.

During the course of writing any story, I always generate ideas for other stories and will often stop the first one to get something on paper about the second. Before that first story is complete, it may have developed a third and a fourth.

Much of my thinking during this period was done on my evening walks, usually along the road but often into a small forest of blackjack nearby. It was a quiet place where nobody ever came. I have always enjoyed wild country, even so small a patch as this, which was, I believe, some three hundred acres.

I continued to review books, which gave me a good opportunity to see what the publishers were buying and what was being read. I reviewed *Young Joseph* by Thomas Mann, *Of Time and the River* by Thomas Wolfe, *Israfel* by Hervey Allen (which I consider the best biography I have read on Edgar Allan Poe), and a good dozen other books.

Additionally, I read several plays by Shakespeare, *Persian Letters* by Montesquieu, and works by Erskine Caldwell, John Millington Synge, and John Galsworthy.

Of Time and the River impressed me, but I thought Thomas Wolfe more the poet than the novelist. His stories made up a long autobiography that no doubt many enjoyed, but his descriptions of train journeys, of October sweeping over the land from Maine to the Carolinas, were sheer poetry. In many ways he saw our country better than anyone else has and caught some moments every traveler has experienced. The chances are he might not have achieved success without the editing of Maxwell Perkins, but one shudders to think what must have been left out. Wolfe had a way of going on and on when touching on a topic he enjoyed, but his going on and on was better than many a writer's carefully chosen words.

Reviewing books also gave me a chance to read what was written when I could not afford to buy the books. The magazines for which I wrote did not want character so much as action, but as my stories became popular, I slowly injected new elements and began using a language different from what was believed by some to be the way western people talked.

The pulp magazines never realized that cowboys came from everywhere, and that the West was a great melting pot of drifters, soldiers of fortune (five of the men who died with Custer had been members of the Vatican Guard, including Captain Keough), and adventurers, the bulk of whom were Anglo-Saxon and Irish, as were the pioneers.

Yet I learned much. A pulp story had to start fast and it had to move, and above all, you had to have a story to tell.

I have told many, yet when I go down that last trail, I know there will be a thousand stories hammering at my skull, demanding to be told.

And I am amply repaid when any old-timer, and there have been many, can put his finger on a line and say, "Yes, that is the way it was."

No choicer gift can any man give to another than his spirit's intimate converse with itself.
— SCHLEIERMACHER

17

In pursuing my education, I had been reading approximately one hundred books per year. By that I mean books completed, and it says nothing of those I dipped into or simply referred to from time to time. Yet I was continually disturbed by the fact that our histories seemed to begin with Egypt and Mesopotamia and to progress from there to Greece, Rome, the rest of Europe, and then North America. The remainder of the world seemed only marginal and of no interest.

Rich as our Western literature was, I wished to learn more about Asia and Africa. My travels had made me realize how much there was to learn. Wherever I could, I would find students who would give me sight translations of books or simply relate the stories of their people. In this way I first heard some of the many chapters of the *Shahnama*, Iran's great Book of Kings. The entire epic contains much of the history of Iran (Persia) as well as some of its fabulous folk tales. I now have in my library the Reuben Levy translation, which I believe to be the best.

Usually finding such students was a simple matter of locating the coffeehouses they preferred and getting to know them. They were excited by my interest and they enjoyed telling the stories. Of course I bought the coffee. It was a cheap tuition for all I was learning.

There were many translations from Asiatic works, but as a rule they did not fall into the path of the average reader, nor were they studied in school. The works of Confucius, Mencius, and some of the other philosophers and poets could be found. Early on I had read Harold Lamb's biographies of Genghis Khan and Tamerlane, which were available in most libraries and had a good readership (as did most of his books), but they were exceptions.

The tales of the *Shah-nama* are still told along the caravan trails with some minor variations here and there, as are stories of that other hero of Central Asia and Tibet, Kesar of Ling. The man who first told me of Kesar was a murderer and a thief, a bandit by choice, occasional employee of archaeological expeditions, and a good friend when I needed one.

Within the past few years, we in the Western world have benefited (if we would have it so), by one of the greatest works any man or group of men ever attempted. I refer to James Needham and his associates, who have put together the multivolume *Science and Civilization in China*. Although I have every volume published thus far, I have not read them all, nor, to be frank, am I anxious to. I much prefer to dip into them here or there and follow some particular idea or theme. Each book is a treasure, astonishing in its breadth and scope, and I find myself trying to make each one last. I have felt this way as well about the books of Joseph Rock, who made many Far Eastern expeditions for *National Geographic*.

The fiction of China is well worth reading. Tso Hsueh-chin's *Hung Lou Menq*, known in English as *Dream of the Red Chamber*, is one of China's finest novels. It is perhaps the best picture of Chinese life and society that one can find. *Outlaw's of the Marsh*, written of twelfth-century events and translated by Pearl Buck in a somewhat abbreviated version as *All Men Are Brothers*, is one of the most exciting. The Sidney Schapiro translation is the one I prefer.

Two Chinese classics which I liked very much were *The Scholars* and *The Romance of Three Kingdoms*, and I found the *Travels of Lao Ts'an* a delight.

The world with which Americans must deal in the future will no longer be confined to that small area called Europe, although its importance will continue. We must take heed of India and China, of Pakistan and Southeast Asia. The key to understanding any people is in its art: its writing, painting, sculpture. The people of China have ever been intelligent, inventive, and industrious, and if they can cope with their population problem, they will again be the power they once were.

Due to the narrow vision in many of our schools, few of our people have any knowledge of or appreciation for the culture of Asiatic nations. There has been a slight change for the better in recent years but our people are still relatively uninformed. Too many believe nothing was known of China until Marco Polo returned with his stories.

As a matter of fact, Seneca had made fiery speeches in the Roman forum protesting the adverse balance of trade with India, and the vast sums in gold that were being sent to purchase Indian goods. Some historians have even gone so far as to suggest it was one of the reasons for the decline and fall of the Roman Empire. Certainly it was for some years a contributing factor.

There were several ports on the Red Sea coast of Egypt where ships were constantly sailing for India — at the rate of one per day in the 120-day sailing season, when winds were favorable. Ships in those days in most places did not come alongside a dock to discharge cargo, but were run ashore at high tide and unloaded when the water receded. At Myos Hormos, one of those ports, the old foundations still exist.

Ambassadors were sent by Rome to the courts of India and China, or in some cases people represented themselves as such. Troupes of acrobats and actors had traveled from Rome to China, and plays were performed in Greece using phrases from the language of Ceylon. And there is good evidence that an entire Roman legion sold its services to the Chinese and served as mercenary soldiers in many of their wars.

Nations are born, they mature, grow old, and almost die, but after some years they rise again, and we in this country, as in all nations, need leaders with vision. Too few can see further than the next election and will agree to spend any amount of money as long as some of it is spent in the area they represent. H. G. Wells wisely said that "Men who think in lifetimes are of no use to statesmanship."

Now, with the vast distances of space opening before us, and the length of the journeys into outer space, we must begin to think in terms of generations and centuries rather than in years. Even with increased speeds and ease of travel, many of the exploratory journeys will be long.

It may also be important to consider trying to return some of the planets to livable worlds. We have many plants on earth that live in extreme deserts or on the fringes of icecaps, surviving under seemingly impossible conditions. Such plants might be given a trial in likely spots — and leave the rest to time.

There is evidence that there once was water on Mars, and very likely there are ice caves in some of the lava beds, just as we have on this earth.

As I have said elsewhere, I believe that all that has gone before has been but preliminary, that our real history began with that voyage to the moon. Progress at first may be slow, but man will not be held back. There will always be those few who wish to push back the frontiers, to see what lies beyond.

As much time as I have spent in cities, walking

and working among people of all kinds, I liked the wild country the best. Again and again I returned to the desert or the mountains, seeking out the lonely water holes, studying the wild life, learning to exist on the outer margins. Given paper with which to write and a typewriter, I can be happy anywhere.

When writing of the American West, we need take nothing for granted. Gunfighters, buffalo hunters, Indians, Army officers, and all manner of pioneers have told their stories, and not a few excellent books have been written by women or about women in the West.

During the Roosevelt administration the Federal Writers' Project sent out people to interview old-timers and gather what material they could. Most of this material lies in Historical Society archives, uncatalogued and unused. The interviews vary in quality, but some are excellent and most contain information important to history.

Joseph McCoy's *Historic Sketches of the Cattle Trade of the West and Southwest* is an excellent book and one of the basic books on that aspect of the west. J. Frank Dobie's *The Longhorns* is another, but it is difficult to begin to list authoritative sources, for there are so many.

There are some years where my reading record is incomplete or nonexistent, but nonetheless I was reading, especially books that took place at sites I was visiting. My wife often says she has driven every back road in the West, and certainly she has driven many of them, roads often taken on a moment's whim. Each was a voyage of discovery, offering new views of the country.

Little by little, I was finding my way into foreign literatures and finding them rich and rewarding. Long before the appearance of samurai films in this country I knew their stories, and that, too, happened in a strange way.

One night in Kobe, Japan, several of us had come ashore. It being too late for me to seek out more interesting places, I was having a beer with my shipmates in the bar.

The owner (or perhaps the manager) was present, friendly, and seated with us. One of the seamen who had come ashore with us was a mean, disagreeable drunk, and for some time he had been muttering to himself about one of the waiters. After a moment he stood up and shoved him so that the man fell. When the owner objected, the seaman hit him with what is often described as a bolo punch, a looping right hand to the groin, and the owner, a much smaller, slighter man, fell to the floor.

We all objected to what had happened and I expressed my feelings in no uncertain terms, so he attacked me. The man was no fighter and what followed could not be described as a fight. The seaman in question was foolish enough to throw a punch at me, but a wild one any child could have avoided. I did so and kicked his feet from under him. When he tried to get up, I pushed him down again and told him to stay until he could behave himself.

He did so, but about that time several very husky young Japanese men came in, and the owner later told me that, had I not coped with the man myself, those young Japanese were prepared to do so.

Finally, I let him get up and he went away, stopping at the door to say, "Some day aboard ship, I'll get you."

As I am writing this many years later, it is obvious that he didn't.

However, the brief difficulty led to a discussion of judo, kung fu, and the various martial arts. That led to a tour of some of the places where they were taught, and I heard for the first time the story of Musashi, said to be the greatest Japanese swordsman.

The owner was very well versed in Japanese history and several times in the next few days we spent time discussing the history of Japan, of *bushido*,* and what it meant to be a samurai.

The story of *Miyamoto Musashi*, as told by Yoshikawa in the Charles Terry translation, is recommended to those interested. There is much material on the samurai period, and perhaps the best history of Japan is the three-volume study by George Sansom. Those who read these lines must understand that I do not claim to be an authority. I simply record what I have found to be interesting, informative, and historically accurate.

*The code of the samurai, which stresses loyalty, obedience, and the valuing of honor above life.

Although my time in Japan was all too brief, I did form some interesting contacts and was fortunate to find, in the bar owner, one who was versed in the history of Japanese martial arts, and in the legends of the samurai and the *bushido* code.

One thing I have discovered about research: Let people know what you are looking for. Often the best information will come from the least likely sources. On one occasion when I was seeking information, and official sources had nothing to offer beyond a few sentences, the porter in my hotel introduced me to a man who had all the facts, and was one of the people whom I was investigating. Had I depended upon official sources or libraries, I would have left the country knowing nothing more than had been printed for years. As it was, a door was opened for me and I learned a great deal.

No possible source should be despised, yet I have known some very bright people who ignored any but official sources. I admit that careful checking is necessary, but often that is easily done, once the basic facts are known. In one case I wished to locate a ruined stage station. I was told there was no such place, only to learn from a cowboy eating hotcakes in the next booth that every cowhand in the country knew where it was. He met me the next morning, let the fence down, and guided me to the place. Not only that, but he hunkered down on his haunches and told me his great-grandfather had helped to rebuild the place after it had been burned by Indians.

Amazing things can happen, and I know of a case where one individual has almost succeeded in changing history because of his strongly held opinions and his ability to convince others (two of whom have written books) that he is right.

In this case, this gentleman read accounts of the Hole-in-the-Wall in Wyoming, and when he found it to be other than he expected, he decided the facts were wrong. He had a mental picture of its being a small opening, while, as a matter of fact, the Hole is over a quarter of a mile wide with a good creek flowing through.

This was the Hole-in-the-Wall where rustlers drove herds of stolen cattle through and vanished into the country beyond, then drifted from ranch to ranch until out of the country. For years, no posse attempted to go through, as a couple of men with rifles up on the sandstone ridge could make passage impossible or costly.

Not finding what he expected, the gentleman ordered that a search be made; a difficult horse trail, over which cattle could hardly be driven, was discovered. This trail was used only a few times by the outlaws and at least once by Marshal Joe LeFors, who mentions it, and its difficulty, in his own book. But every old-timer knew the real Hole-in-the-Wall was the wide opening referred to above.

The authors of both books should have checked their sources more carefully. The Hole is the only real opening in the Wall for thirty-five miles or so, and the area beyond it was inhabited by rustlers or those friendly to them. (Or if not friendly, in no position to make enemies.)

18

My careful study of the short story and how it was written paid off. As I had many stories to tell, I sold quite a few, although the prices were low and one had to write a lot to make a living.

My one wish was to make my work increasingly better, and here and there I tried to change some editorial beliefs. For example, for some ungodly reason it had long been an established policy that "you" be written in a western story as "yuh." This irritated me and I began to insist on "you." As my stories were increasingly popular, it was usually allowed to stand.

There has been comment from time to time, usually by people with little discernment, on the lack of sex in my stories.

It is very simple. I am not writing about sex, which is a leisure activity; I am writing about men and women who were settling a new country, finding their way through a maze of difficulties, and learning to survive despite them.

Sex in the time before World War I was a private concern, and there were, supposedly, only two places for it: in the bedrooms of married people and in whorehouses. A woman who transgressed was soon known and found herself cut off from society, accepted nowhere. If she did not become a prostitute, she lived on a back street, kept by somebody and isolated from most of society.

There were, of course, sad cases where women for one reason or another acquired a false label, and their lives were ruined by it. Attitudes toward sex can change very quickly and what may be accepted in one generation is condemned in another, or vice versa.

My stories are not concerned with sex but with entering, passing through, or settling wild country. I am concerned with people building a nation, learning to live together, with establishing towns, homes, and bridges to the future.

Those unfamiliar with the world's literature might find it interesting to realize that sex, except in its romantic sense, has little to do with seventy-five percent of what has been written.

My greatest complaint with present-day sexual writing is that nobody seems to be having any fun. Sex is an ordeal, or it is rape, or an athletic endeavor. Only the French find it amusing — as it certainly is. Many of those who choose it for subject matter linger on the most unpleasant aspects or treat it like a discovery. Actually, they needn't. It's been here all the time.

Most people who are familiar with my work think of me as a novelist, but actually I began with short stories, poetry, and a few articles and essays. My apprenticeship as a writer was in the field of the short story, however, and my first novel was written only after selling more than a hundred short stories.

The first novel I had published appeared in England and was called *Westward The Tide*. It did not appear in this country until Bantam Books acquired the rights from me many years later.

Usually I am characterized as a western writer. I do not mind the term, but it is not strictly correct. To me, and to many others, I am a writer of the frontier, not only in the West but elsewhere. Wherever there is a frontier, I am interested; wherever there is a frontier, I am concerned. Much of my writing has to do with men on the western frontier, even when that frontier was east of the Appalachians, as in *Sackett's Land*, *To The Far Blue Mountains*, and *The Warrior's Path*. (Two of these stories begin in Elizabethan England, incidentally, as does *Fair Blows The Wind*.)

The frontier is that line beyond which man has not been, or where he is only beginning to go. I am, for example, concerned now (as I have been since I was twelve) about the frontiers of outer space, and I have appeared several times as a speaker on programs connected with the space movement. This is the final frontier, the frontier without end, and those who explore it will be heroes of the future. There are endless frontiers out there, each one difficult, each one offering fresh discoveries, unexpected challenges, and rewards beyond belief.

My novel *The Walking Drum* is the story of Kerbouchard, a young man seeking the frontiers of knowledge, seeking his fortune as well as wisdom in a rapidly changing world. The twelfth century was one of impending change. The Renaissance had not begun but all the elements were there, and the world in the West was about to burst with creativity like the sudden opening of a flower.

Kerbouchard is himself an instrument in that change. He goes into the Arab world, which holds the center of the world's intellectual activity, and he returns to what is still Dark Ages Europe, talking, listening, relating. He gives a book to a student in Paris, a rare and wonderful gift where books of any kind were rare. He expresses dissenting ideas, and it is no matter whether they are important, simply that they offer a different viewpoint and so are an incentive to thinking.

The merchant caravans of which he is a part are also a piece of what is happening. Traveling from country to country, bound by no boundaries, they carry ideas as well as the goods they sell, and ideas bring questions. Those who have witnessed the rich intellectual lives in the Moslem world are no longer content with the world in which they live. They have looked upon beauty and they wish to create beauty for themselves.

Too often reviewers approaching one of my stories think "he writes adventure stories" and so they see nothing else.

This book began as an account of how I educated myself, but it has often wandered far afield. Yet I have ever been a wanderer, drifting through fields of books and finding blossoms wherever they might bloom. Education is everywhere, prompting one to think, to consider, to remember.

That most fabulous of instruments, the human mind, has never realized its potential in any man, coming closest perhaps in Leonardo da Vinci or Avicenna. The memory, which is now often replaced by computers, notebooks, or whatever, has never been so useful since the Middle Ages, when any Arab (by that I mean anyone, of any nationality, who was a part of the Arab civilization) author could recite the contents of his entire list of books, verbatim. Each author had the text of all of his books committed to memory and would dictate when a book was needed. Druid priests and storytellers everywhere had fabulous memories, for there was no other way. (To those who might question this, I refer them to *The Arabic Book* by Johannes Pedersen as the quickest of many references.)

Someone has said that culture is what remains with you after you have forgotten all you have read, and I believe there is much truth in that.

As I worked in one field, I continued to reach out to others. My short story "The Admiral" appeared in *Story* and received some favorable comment. Edward J. O'Brien, who at the time put together collections of *The Best Short Stories* each year, listed several of mine in his *Index of Distinctive Stories*. Few saw these listings and fewer cared, but they were important to me. Moreover, they were seen by publishers, and several wrote suggesting I might have a book.

Of course I had a book. I have always had a book, but nothing then on paper.

Some correspondence followed and the future looked bright. Then the War came.

It had been going on, of course, and I had followed developments with interest. In my book reviewing, I had handled most of the military and naval books and several on foreign affairs. Our military leaders were admirers of German might, and many were suggesting victory in Russia. I knew that was impossible.

Charles XII of Sweden and Napoleon had both failed, and the Germans had failed to take Leningrad, one of the most exposed cities in the world. The conclusion was obvious to me. When the Russians wished to make a stand, they could and would.

German supply lines stretched out and out and were vulnerable to guerrilla attacks. More men and equipment were needed to supply the fighting men than Germany could get on the line. The Russians had again traded space for time, and moved factories back into Siberia. They were waiting when the Germans arrived, and at Leningrad they stopped them.

Several years before, we in the United States had put on the first mass parachute drops and had promptly done nothing with them; in France a colonel named De Gaulle had written a book on *The Army of the Future* in which he outlined a mechanized army which was to be adopted, with minor changes, as the panzer division. Major General J.F.C. Fuller had written *Field Service Regulations III* in which he laid down the plan for blitzkreig warfare. The French were committed to a war of position and did nothing with De Gaulle's motorized division; the British had other ideas and ignored Fuller's concept. The Germans saw the value in all three ideas and used them.

(A Frenchman — a correspondent, I believe — who was in Germany during the early days of the Hitler takeover heard much talk of a French military genius. He was surprised, as he did not know they had one, and the Germans told him of De Gaulle. Returning to France, he made queries and located him for an interview.)

Having considerable knowledge of what is now Indonesia, Malaysia, and the China coast, I tried for Naval Intelligence. It was there I believed I might be most useful, and that was what I wanted most. However, without a college degree, I was turned down.

Often when one hears of war memories, one would believe the teller of the stories directed his own destiny. None of us did. We went where we were told to go and did what we were told to do, and that is the way with armies. I did many things, but only twice, for brief periods, was I in a position where my experience was useful, and neither lasted long.

My basic training was in the Infantry at Camp Robinson, and from there to Officers' Candidate

School at Camp Hood, Texas, in the Tank Destroyers. For a time after graduation I was involved in various training activities, more or less routine stuff, until several of us were sent north from Camp McCoy, Wisconsin, to the northern peninsula of Michigan as instructors in winter survival.

This was one of the jobs for which I was thoroughly equipped. Growing up in North Dakota, I understood cold, and several times in Oregon I had taken a rifle or a shotgun and gone into the woods in the depth of winter to spend a week or more just knocking about and camping out. Such forays had taught me a great deal about survival in the cold, so I was well equipped as an instructor.

However, it was on my military record that I had been to sea. Whether it was for that reason or not, I never knew, but I was shipped to San Francisco to become, briefly again, a cargo control officer.

Again, this was a job for which I was equipped. Not only had I gone to sea and studied cargo stowage, but I had worked as a longshoreman, and was personally acquainted with some of the waterfront bosses. It was a job where I could get things done, and I was scheduled after some brief time on the San Francisco waterfront to go out to the Pacific islands in that capacity.

What I wanted was action. When I chose Tank Destroyer school over Infantry school it was because it promised action and movement. At Kasserine Pass and elsewhere there had been a heavy loss of personnel, so men were needed. Yet I had to admit that what they planned for me was something I could do and, due to previous experience, knew I could do well. I took my shots, packed my gear, and got ready to return to the familiar waters of the Pacific. I knew the people out there, knew the islands, knew I could be useful.

So what happened?

A group of officers were scheduled to go east to join various units, and one of them fell ill. The officer who had been planning my future was off duty, a sergeant in charge put me on the list, and paid no attention to my protests.

My arguments failed to sway him and he could find nothing that implied I was to ship out to the Pacific. His orders demanded so many officers, and as I was available, I was to be one of them.

My protests did no good, so I relaxed. Perhaps the man was saving my life. Maybe the destination for which I was headed in the Pacific would be destroyed by an enemy attack. One pushed his luck just so far, so I bent with the Army wind.

As it turned out, my time overseas was spent in the European Theater of Operations. I did what I was given to do and they gave me four Bronze Stars for doing it reasonably well. I spent time in England before D-Day, traveled in France, Belgium, the Netherlands, Luxembourg, and Germany and made some good friends in France who are my friends still.

There was no time for writing during the war,

but one could always think, and one could observe and remember. The beach at Brignogan from which Kerbouchard was taken into slavery I first saw at this time, with its white sands and stark black rocks. On a brief vacation, one of the few times when I was free, I visited a castle in the forest, now a ruined castle of stone, but in *The Walking Drum* it was built of timber, as most of them were. This was the castle where Kerbouchard killed his enemy Tournemine and from which he took his body to dump it into what was believed to be the mouth of Hell.

There were places and people to be seen and remembered, there were stories to be heard, and I was hungry for them all. Ours is a rich and wonderful world, and there are stories everywhere. Nobody should ever try to second-guess history; the facts are fantastic enough.

The Armed Services editions of books in paperback were sent along with rations, and I read many. Our company put on a show at one time in which various soldiers did takeoffs on the officers, most of them remarkably good. The big fellow who did me came onto the stage with his pockets stuffed with books.

Earth has not anything to show more fair:
Dull would he be of soul who could pass by
A sight so touching in its majesty:
This City now doth, like a garment, wear
The beauty of the morning; silent, bare,
Ships, towers, domes, theatres, and temples
   lie
Open unto the fields, and to the sky;
All bright and glittering in the smokeless air.
Never did sun more beautifully steep
In his first splendour, valley, rock, or hill;
Ne'er saw I, never felt, a calm so deep!
The river glideth at his own sweet will:
Dear God! the very houses seem asleep;
And all that mighty heart is lying still!
           — WILLIAM WORDSWORTH
      Composed upon Westminister Bridge

19

The war was over in Europe and many of my outfit had gone home. I had been switched to another company temporarily and had put in for emergency leave. Surprisingly, it came through and I was directed to Le Havre to return on the U.S.S. *Boise*, a light cruiser.

Several officers from various services were also aboard and we were pleased. The *Boise* usually made the crossing in four to four and half days, I heard, and we would be home in time for Christmas of 1945.

I should have known better. Maybe there is something about me that attracts large storms at sea: on my first voyage we went through a hurricane in the West Indies. Later, I endured two typhoons in the China seas, and was aboard a small ship off the Florida coast when the hurricane ripped Miami in 1926.

The storm the *Boise* encountered was the worst in many years and we needed sixteen days instead of four and a half to make the crossing. An aircraft carrier had to put into the Azores with damage aboard, and the only other vessel to cross during that storm was the *Boise*'s sister ship, the U.S.S. *Reno*.

When paid off and out of the Army, I called Leo Margulies. He was giving a party and I was invited. It was mostly a publishing crowd and somebody — perhaps it was Leo — asked me what I planned.

"To write, of course. I've got to make a living."

"You know the West. Write some westerns and I'll buy them."

Before I left for the Army, I told him, several publishers had wanted books from me and I expected to try that market. Having left the country with everything looking good for me, I expected and hoped to find the situation unchanged. I should have known better.

One editor whom I had known had gone into the foreign service (or so I heard), another into the Navy. The entire regimes at some publishing houses had changed completely and I was to find that nobody knew anything about me. Certainly there was no reason why they should, for I had published only a scattering of short stories, most of them in magazines not rated for their literary quality. The few who had shown interest had moved on. In any event, the interest had been tentative and nobody had promised me anything.

Although I had saved a little money during the war, I knew it would not last long. To write was imperative, and not only to write but to sell.

There was a market for western stories, and I had grown up on them. I had worked on ranches, in mines and lumber camps, and had covered a lot of the western country in one way or another.

I thought I knew the West, but I had much to learn.

To those who have not researched the field, it is difficult to grasp the extent of factual written material available. Moreover, there are photographs of cowboys themselves, of trail herd crews, saloons, western streets, ranches, line cabins, anything you might wish to see.

Most of the gunfighters were photographed at one time or another, so good pictures are available, as well as some fine pictures of Indians, Indian villages, and war parties.

I reread *The Log of a Cowboy* by Andy Adams, who had been over the trail with cattle; read *Trail Drivers of Texas* (one of the basic books), *Tales of the Mustangs*, and *A Vaquero of the Brush Country* by J. Frank Dobie. In that first year I read thirty-two books on various aspects of western history, including biographies of Bill Tilghman, Captain Bill McDonald, Dave Cook, Wild Bill Hickok, as well as *The Last of the Bandit Riders* by Matt Warner, who had ridden with Butch Cassidy among others, and *Army Life on the Border* by Gen. Randolph B. Marcy, who explored much of the West. He also wrote the best guidebook to crossing the plains by the various routes, with distances, water holes, and so on.

There was also an excellent biography of *Jeff Milton*, by J. Evetts Haley, the *Journal of John Udell*, and *The Overland Route to California* by Andrew Child. These were journals of the westward trip, of which there are many.

My intent then, as always, was to deal with existing historical situations. The old staples of the western — cowboys, rustlers, trail drives, stolen cattle, and ranch feuds — were present, but historically they had been a big part of the picture.

No place I know had the story potential of the West, for stories are about people, and those who went west were strongly individual.

The western pioneers were select people, selected by themselves. They chose to break the mold, to leave all they knew behind and venture into a new country, with new problems, new standards. Each one was expected to stand on his own feet. He was moving of his own volition, on his own support system. Nobody was paying his way or showing him the way; nobody had told him to go, or where to go. He simply packed what goods he could carry and headed west, looking for what chance might offer.

Ours has been called a materialistic society. The Europeans love saying that of us, but I have never found a society that was not materialistic. If you find one, you may be sure it will be dying.

Man seeks a means to exist; then he strives to improve that situation. At first he wants something to eat; then he tries to store food against times of famine. He tries to find warmer furs, a better cave, a more secure life. He creates better weapons with which to defend himself, to form alliances that will assist in his protection. It is a normal, natural thing and has existed forever.

Success often means security, safety in your home, safety in your possessions. To me success has meant just two things: a good life for my family, and the money to buy books and continue the education of this wandering man, who has ceased to wander except in his memory, his thoughts, and the books he writes.

Books are precious things, but more than that, they are the strong backbone of civilization. They are the thread upon which it all hangs, and they can save us when all else is lost.

We do not know how many civilizations have existed before us. One of the greatest, that of the Indus Valley in India, was unknown until 1928, and little was done to investigate its extent until after World War II. Now we know that about 2500 B.C. and later, there existed in India a civilization at least as extensive as that of Egypt, and that it had trade relations with Sumeria, with Ur of the Chaldees.

It is possible there was a thin line of connection stretching all the way from the Minoan civilization of Crete to Egypt, Sumeria, Dilmun, the Indus Valley and China in 2500 B.C., give or take five hundred years. What other civilizations are yet to be discovered we do not know, but I believe several will be found, one of them in the Taklamakan Desert of Sinkiang in western China, or somewhere in that vast area that once was called Chinese Turkestan.

We are only beginning to discover what South America holds for us, but new finds are constantly being made and the areas of civilization are being extended.

The necessities of exploring the history and literature of the American West did not close other doors for me. Much of the study of history is a matter of comparison, of relating what was happening in one area to what was happening elsewhere, and what had happened in the past. To view a period in isolation is to miss whatever message it has to offer.

We view the devastation of Hiroshima with horror, but such things happened regularly in the ancient world. The Assyrians destroyed every major city in their region several times over, with body counts far exceeding that at Hiroshima, and Tamerlane made pyramids of the skulls of those destroyed in his westward march. The tide of civilization was turned back again and again by the march of barbarians, and unhappily some of the barbarians came from within the civilization itself.

The study of history has taken a turn for the better in the last few years, with less concern for wars and politics than for the life of the people, their manner of living, and the world in which they lived. Fernand Braudel, Daniel Boorstin, and Henri Pirenne (to name a few) have opened the way to a better understanding of how men lived, worked, created and discovered. It is a most healthy transition.

As I was researching the American West, I was also delving into the histories of India, China, and Southeast Asia. That Arab boy, long ago in Indonesia, had no idea what he started, but I owe him a debt. He opened a door for me that has never closed.

I often say that a writer owes a debt of authenticity to his readers. Because of his profession he may go to the fountains of knowledge and drink as deeply as he wishes. This is not given to all people who are concerned with making a living and providing services, and writers are the go-betweens. Readers wish to believe the printed word, God help them, and I believe when we deal with history or anything factual, it should be with care. We may be the only source they have for such information. Once the real-life situation is established, we can take off in any direction we wish. If a story is to be fantasy — and I love it — that should be obvious from word one.

A writer of stories, such as I have been and am, is expected to entertain. I have my corner in the marketplace where, like the storytellers of the Arabian Nights or the minstrels and bards of bygone years, I tell my stories. To entertain, for me, is not enough. I have drunk deep of those fountains and I would share what I have learned. There is, woven into the texture of what I hope are entertaining tales, a good bit of how people lived, what they thought, and how they survived in desert, mountain, and city. Nietzsche said it best when he wrote (as I recall), "I have a song to sing and will sing it, although I am alone in an empty house and must sing to my own ears."

It is not enough to have learned, for living is

sharing and I must offer what I have for whatever it is worth.

I shall do an autobiography, perhaps as fiction — which I write best — but it will be true. The early years were harder than anyone can imagine and what I have written here in some of the early chapters just skims the surface of what was happening. It is never easy to be hungry, never easy to be alone, never easy to believe in oneself when nobody else does.

The rough times were made smoother by the realization that it was all grist for the mill, and that someday I would be writing, with knowledge, of what I was experiencing then. I had that advantage over many others who traveled the same road.

As I continued studying the West, I came to know the country I had seen through other eyes, to view it as women in covered wagons saw it, as children did, and as did the husbands and fathers, daring yet frightened men, awestruck at what they had done yet determined to carry it through.

A journey is time suspended. All decisions await arrival, and one travels on, day after day, accepting each as it comes. At the end is the harsh reality of decision and doing. Reading through the old journals, one begins to read between the lines and sense the doubt, the hope, the fear of what lies ahead.

To read one diary is something. In reading fifty, you become a part of their world and cannot escape. The people on the march become your friends, and you know how they feel. The diaries are not only of the westward march; many are of life on lonely claims, isolated from all but a few scattered neighbors.

Somewhere about this time or a bit later I read Washington Irving's *A Tour on the Prairies*, Will Hale's *Twenty-four Years a Cowboy and Ranchman*, and James Cook's *Fifty Years on the Old Frontier*. Following that, I read Daniel Jones's *Forty Years Among Wild Indians*, *The History of Kanauj* by Dr. R. S. Tripathi, *Beast and Man in India* by Lockwood Kipling (the father of Rudyard, who wrote a number of books himself), and *Ruins of Desert Cathay* in two thick volumes by Sir Aurel Stein.

Particularly fascinating to me was the study of the discoveries made by Stein along the ruins of the Great Wall of China at its farthest westward extension, the fragments of poetry written on bamboo by lonely soldiers, many of whom were sent to duty in the far west of China as boys and returned only as old men no longer fit to serve.

It was never a part of my nature to focus on one area to the detriment of others. I wished to understand it all, and to have a clear picture in my mind of what was happening in all parts of the world. And wherever I could, I listened to the stories along caravan trails, in bars, coffee- or teahouses, and wherever they might be heard.

My friend the bandit, whom I mentioned earlier, discovered very quickly where my interests lay and made it his business to find and bring to me people with stories to tell. Always he sat by, that gifted man of many languages, ready to translate or to fill in gaps, even to explain some aspect of geography pertaining to the story's locale.

When the icy winds sweep down from the peaks of that most mysterious of mountain ranges, the Kuen-lun, the camel-dung fires blaze up briefly, then smolder and smoke, and the dust of thousands of years stirs along what once was the Silk Road from China to the West. The voices around the fire grow still and men listen into the night for the passing of ghost caravans traveling to ghost cities lost in the Taklamakan.

It is a time for stories, a time for listening.

20

Those who have never ventured away from the security of their cities, their diplomatic corps, or their business relationships must understand that there is a half-world out there, a place that lies beyond the pale of the law or fringing it: a world of people who move about, cross borders, lose themselves in crowds; a half-world that knows where illegal papers can be obtained, visas, licenses, whatever is necessary.

One comes to it easily if one mingles with that sort of people, those who live on the fringe. There are ways to pass borders, to avoid checkpoints, and to exist away from the eyes of officials. I am sure it is not as easy as it once was, but I am equally sure it goes on still.

Occasionally word comes to me from one of the old crowd, but their ranks are thinning. In every large seaport city there were places one might go to meet people of like interests. Some men dealt in guns and munitions, some in information, and others were smugglers of goods or of people. Still others merely wished to avoid the eyes of officials in going wherever it was they wished to go, and some had no means of obtaining the proper papers and so used other means.

It was Oriental Slim in San Pedro who first put me in touch, and advised me where to go in Shanghai, Hong Kong, Tientsin, and Saigon. Later I knew such places in a dozen other cities and went to them to meet people, to soak up atmosphere, and just to hear what was happening along the outside routes.

Slim had fought in several armies but had settled down to shacking up with native girls of whatever country he was in, and staying drunk much of the time. When I met him, he was on one of his extended periods of sobriety, and as I was never a drinker, we had many long talks.

My first contact in Shanghai came in a sailors' joint called, if I remember correctly, the Olympic, having nothing to do with the Games — although games of other kinds were played there.

It was a perhaps-accidental meeting with a Scotsman, a former British-India Army officer named Haig. He had left the service and become a Buddhist, but I always suspected he was with British Intelligence.

We talked, and he knew of Slim. He introduced me to a young couple, brother and sister, who were half-castes. They had an independent income from somewhere — not a lot of money, but security. She painted, Chinese-style; he wrote very elegant poetry which he rarely tried to publish.

Through them, and at several parties, I became acquainted with a small group of would-be artists and writers, mostly half-castes. Markets for what they wrote not existing, they simply wrote for their mutual pleasure — although the sister who painted occasionally sold something of hers. Indeed, a few years ago I came upon a painting of hers in a home I was visiting, but the owners had no idea who the artist was, and I did not enlighten them. They had come upon a charming piece of work and bought it for no other reason.

I knew the young half-castes for a few days only, and since have heard they were in Nanking when the Japanese came. It is hardly to be expected that they escaped. Haig would have, and Slim if sober, but the artists were flowers that bloomed in the spring and can scarcely have escaped the first freeze.

Our world is made up of a myriad of microcosms, of tiny worlds, each with its own habitués, every one known to the others. A neighborhood bar or café can be a comforting place to go, to talk with friends or acquaintances, people unknown just a few blocks away. Often, driving down a street, I notice such places and am tempted to drop in, listen, and enter briefly another small world people have created for themselves.

In some neighborhoods it is not a good idea at all, and better you should keep driving.

Many people have the idea that a writer of stories should live in the area of which he writes, but if he knows his subject matter, he carries it with him wherever he goes. Much of my life has been spent in deserts and mountains; much of what I have seen I remember. Sitting here now, I can close my eyes and see the desert in all its many aspects. There is no need to see it again, although I often shall, nor is there need to go to the mountains, for the mountains are with me always. I have walked the high country; I have breathed its air, bedded down under its trees, watched the white clouds drift and the storm clouds gather. Far away I have seen dust-devils do their weird dance and I have heard the pelting rain on the trees above me.

I remember the decks of ships where I have walked, the feel of the wheel in my hands, the drip of water from yellow oilskins, and I have heard the crash of great trees coming down in the forest. One does not have to live among these things to remember them, and I do. They were and are a part of me.

Indeed, I find that distance lends perspective and I often write better of a place when I am some distance from it. One can be so overwhelmed by the forest as to miss seeing the trees.

Even now, after so many years, I can close my eyes and feel that old E. K. Wood Lumber Dock where the steam schooners lay in their slips, waiting to discharge their cargo of timber from Grays Harbor or somewhere to the north. I can feel the dampness of fog on my face, see the lights of loading ships across the channel on the old Luckenbach dock, and hear the deep-throated blast of a whistle on a steamer outward bound for the far places.

One does not forget the dark, lonely nights, or the odd little memories that linger for no specific reason.

The worlds of which I write are no longer out there. They are here, ever present in my mind. Seated at my typewriter, I can in one moment move to the mountains of Pakistan or India, to vast invading armies with their forests of spears, all bright and golden in the noonday sun. I have read the history; I know the land. I know how it feels to be a fighting man entering combat, so I can ride with those men, fight beside them, fall to the field and lie wounded or die with them.

A writer is bound by no earthly ties; what he is and what he sees he creates in his mind, or his subconscious creates it for him. Thanks to the lands I have seen and the books I have read, I know what it was like. The world of which I write is my world always. It is a claim I have staked and continue to stake, and each writer has his own way of telling a story.

When at the typewriter I am no longer where I sit but am away across the mountains, in ancient cities or on the Great Plains among the buffalo. Often I think of what pitiful fools are those who use mind-altering drugs to seek feelings they do not have, each drug taking a little more from what they have of mind, leaving them a little less. Give the brain encouragement from study, from thinking, from visualizing, and no drugs are needed.

My reading continued, as always, in many areas: *The Ethno-Botany of the Cahuilla Indians* by David Prescott Barrows, *Pioneer Days in Arizona* by Frank Lockwood, *My Sixty Years on the Plains* by William T. Hamilton, *The Vedic Age* by Majumdar and Pulsalker, *The Art of Teaching* by Gilbert Highet, *Rome Beyond Imperial Frontiers* by Sir Mortimer Wheeler, and many another.

I had taken to dropping in at the Brown Derby on Vine Street in Hollywood. Cobb, who operated the place, had connections among the Crow Indians in Wyoming and Montana and we often talked about that country. There was a group of us who gathered at the corner of the bar to talk about motion pictures, writing, the West, and whatever came to mind. One night I told a story of some happenings during World War II, and a few months later it appeared in a motion picture called *Red Ball Express* with my role, much exaggerated, played by Jeff Chandler.

Other than those occasional evenings at the Derby, my time was divided between the Hollywood library and my typewriter.

As I wrote the stories I could sell, I was like a squirrel, gathering the nuts of future stories and storing them for the years when my writing would be better and my market larger.

My first motion picture was *East of Sumatra*, with Jeff Chandler, Anthony Quinn, and Marilyn Maxwell. The story was of tin mining, and made a bit of sense as written. A big company was rushing in to exploit an island ruled by a native Rajah, played by Quinn. He wanted a hospital, medicines, and doctors for his people. The Company wanted to get in and get the tin and get out with as little trouble as possible. The idea was good, the cast was capable — and instead of a meaningful picture, the producers or somebody turned it into a sex and jungle epic.

In any jungle picture with a beautiful native girl, you can almost be sure that before long you will find her swimming naked or nearly so in a pool, usually with a waterfall, and there the leading man comes upon her. He is often in the pool himself, and it leads to what is expected to be a titillating scene. So it was in this case. The sincere young Rajah is largely forgotten, he doesn't get his medicines, and his hopes and the picture go down the drain.

As I delved deeper into the background of America, I became tantalized by the unwritten chapters, most of which we will never know because the information simply is not there. Of course, there is always the chance that in old records in England, France, or Spain we may turn up stories now unknown.

The records we have are those of known explorations, but what of the many that were unknown? In doing research one stumbles upon tantalizing tidbits, mentions of white men living with Indians in areas where no white men were known to be, mentions of boatloads of Carolina adventurers at the mouth of the Ohio a hundred years before Daniel Boone was born, of that party of French people who went west from Illinois to Washington before Lewis and Clark's trek over almost the same route. In almost every instance where somebody was supposed to be first, we find there was somebody already there.

No doubt many a lone hunter went west and never returned; no doubt other explorers did the same. We must always understand that what we have is only a small piece of history. Our forefathers were a restless, venturesome lot and that vast land to the westward, beyond the far blue mountains, was always a challenge.

To understand what happened in our country it is enough to read the major histories, which follow the main lines of thought and of our affairs, but to get down to the nitty-gritty, one must go to the lesser-known books, the pamphlets, the individual memoirs.

There are local histories also, histories of small towns, of counties, of areas important to the writers of the booklets or articles. Newspapers frequently ran the life stories of local pioneers, and they are often valuable additions to the larger pages of history. The story of Robert E. Lee as a young officer, facing the Indian Wildcat and his band, is one I have not seen in any biography of Lee.

My reading continued with *Byzantine Civilization* by Steven Runciman, *Sagebrush Dentist* by Will Frackelton, *History of the Nation of Archers* by Grigor of Akanc, *My Life as an Indian* by J. W. Schultz, *The Secret of the Hittites* by C. W. Ceram, and *Dodge City: The Cowboy Capital* by Robert Wright. Bob Wright was mayor of Dodge in its wild days, and a hide-trader as well.

Frackelton, the dentist mentioned above, once

was asked by a lady gambler to set a diamond in one of her front teeth. As the tooth was healthy and solid he did not wish to, but she insisted. Finally he asked what the idea was, and she replied, "You're a doctor and not supposed to talk about your patients, so I'll tell you. When I'm playing poker I keep my mouth shut, but when I start to deal, I smile." The idea was that, when they were looking at that diamond, they were not watching the cards she was dealing.

Before going overseas to the war, I had met Chris Madsen, a Dane who had done a year in the Danish Army, then seven years in the French Foreign Legion when it was seeing some of its toughest service. Following that, he had come to America and joined the Fifth Cavalry, where, due to his experience, he was immediately made sergeant. I was fortunate enough to talk to him several times. He had been present when Buffalo Bill Cody killed Yellow Hand in a hand-to-hand fight. Cody was a scout for the Fifth at the time and had been challenged before a battle by Yellow Hand.

Chris Madsen lived to be over ninety years old and was a salty, interesting man to the last. He, in company with Bill Tilghman and Heck Thomas, had been one of the Three Musketeers who helped to clean out the outlaw population of the Indian Territory and what became Oklahoma. He was a Deputy United States Marshal at that time.

Bill Tilghman, a gentleman and an honorable man, was one of the best peace officers on the western frontier, respected by his peers. One way of judging how good a man was is by the respect others had for him.

Bob Wright said that if the truth were known, Mysterious Dave Mathers had probably killed more men than any other, yet on one memorable night when he had slain another peace officer in a personal fight, Tilghman went out to arrest him.

Mathers had holed up in an office on the second floor. Tilghman came to the foot of the steps and called up. "Dave? Are you coming down or am I going to have to come up after you?"

Mathers came down.

But for my children, I would have them
   keep their distance from the thickening
   center; corruption
Never has been compulsory, when the cities
   lie at the monster's feet there are left the
   mountains.

— ROBINSON JEFFERS
from "Shine, Perishing Republic"

21

One evening when we were driving across west central Texas we stopped at a ranch house where my companion had once worked as a cowboy. He was now a moderately successful small-business man and interested in promoting some fights.

We stopped to buy a meal, but of course our money was refused, and as the hour grew late we were invited to spend the night.

It was my first experience with a feather bed, but an experience I fought all night long. The trouble was that on the bedside table was a battered copy of Olive R. Dixon's book on her husband, *The Life of Billy Dixon*. At that time the book was scarce (it has since been reprinted) and it was doubtful I would ever see another copy.

The basic facts of Billy Dixon's life were known to me. He had been in the Adobe Walls fight, where twenty-eight buffalo hunters and one woman fought off seven hundred to one thousand Comanche and Kiowa warriors. At that time, Billy shot an Indian off his horse at a distance checked by an army engineer as seven-eighths of a mile.

Billy had also survived the Buffalo Wallow fight, and was famous as a buffalo hunter and as one of the best rifle shots on the frontier, so I very much wanted to know his story. The result was that, despite the feather bed, I managed to stay awake most of the night to finish the story before leaving. As I was very tired, it was something of a struggle, but I completed the book just before sunrise, which was getting-up time. (Recently I reread the book and found it every bit as good as I had remembered.)

Dixon was a man born for the frontier. He came west at fourteen, worked as a teamster, a scout for the Army, and did a lot of hunting and guiding. He survived some incredible storms and took it all without complaint. It was part of the day's work. Going west was a romantic adventure and so it always remained for him.

Whenever I could, I sought out the stories of those who had lived the western adventure, and by comparison could judge the quality and the truth of what I was reading. Times were often very rough for me but I can honestly say I never felt abused or put-upon. I never felt, as some have, that I deserved special treatment from life, and I do not recall ever complaining that things were not better. Often I wished they were, and often found myself wishing for some sudden windfall that would enable me to stop wandering and working and settle down to simply writing. Yet it was necessary to be realistic. Nothing of the kind was likely to happen, and of course, nothing did.

I never found any money; I never won any prizes; I was never helped by anyone, aside from an occasional encouraging word — and those I valued. No fellowships or grants came my way, because I was not eligible for any and in no position to get anything of the sort. I never expected it to be easy.

There was one thing, and one man whom I have not forgotten. At one time, trying desperately to write something that would sell, I rented a typewriter. For several months I paid the rent. Then a time came when I could not, so I wrote him a note and explained. I never heard from him again. No bill, nothing. That typewriter meant more to me than anything else that happened. I was able to go on working.

About that time I first read *Clowning Through Life* by Eddie Foy, who was performing onstage in Dodge City when a drunken cowboy fired some shots through the wall. Foy hit the deck and was narrowly missed. Wyatt Earp and another officer fired at the cowboy, killing him. It was the only Dodge City killing in which Earp figured.

Foy's book is a good one and presents a view of what was happening from another angle. Western men loved theater of any kind, and Foy was very well liked on the frontier. Nearly every town had something resembling a theater, and usually performances were highly successful. There were a number of barnstorming companies touring the West in wagons, performing wherever opportunity offered. Shakespeare was enormously popular, and it was not unusual to hear him quoted at length. John Ringo, that much-overrated gunfighter, would often quote him when drinking.

Another popular form of entertainment in the West was boxing. Prizefighting has gone through many changes in this country, as elsewhere, and there were several years when no decision was permitted. Boxing was legal, but a decision was not. What effect that was supposed to have I never knew, but unless there was a knockout or a win so decisive it could not be questioned, fighters and others waited until the newspapers came out with their decision on who won.

Going through the record books of the 1920–1930 period, one will find "ND" after many of the fights.

Boxing was illegal in several states, including Texas for a time. That is not to say there were no fights. However, because they were illegal, they were held in warehouses, barns, farmyards, anywhere a ring could be set up and a crowd gathered.

In California in the 1920's a bout was limited to four rounds. Hence, the fans expected sheer mayhem in those short fights. Several extra fighters waited, and if you did not throw leather from bell to bell, you were taken out and another fight substituted.

As times changed, so did the fighters. In the beginning, when the Irish were newly arrived or second generation, most of the good fighters were Irish. It was their way out of the streets. Next came the Jews and the Italians, many of them using Irish names, and always there were blacks, and some excellent fighters among them.

Fighters came from everywhere, but the best ones always came out of the ghettos or the mean streets. Many of the boys in the lighter divisions had served their apprenticeship as newsboys fighting to keep a corner where papers sold well. Money was hard to come by and jobs paid little, yet if a boy could fight, he often had a ticket to the top, or hoped he did. Nearly every small town had someone who believed he was a fighter, and some of them were good. Most had never had instruction from anyone who really knew the game, and their reputations had been built on victories over other local fighters.

Many of my fights were in tank towns such as these, where I was a stranger or a new arrival facing a local boy who was often popular. To win at all, one had to win decisively.

Boxing is not what it used to be, and whenever a fighter appears with a long string of knockouts, you may be sure he was fighting bums or men sadly out of condition. It is not easy to knock out a well-conditioned fighter who knows anything about the business. Good fighters can be knocked out, of course, but when one finds twenty or thirty knockouts in a row, you may be sure most of the opponents were not ready for a fight.

At least half of the fighters in the twenties and thirties were fighting under pseudonyms. Many were called "Kid," "Kayo," "Battling," or "Young" — for example: Louis "Kid" Kaplan, Young Stribling, Battling Nelson, among others.

Johnny Dundee, a great featherweight who held the title for a while, was actually an Italian who had been given the Scottish name by his manager, Scotty Monteith. Later, several other Italian fighters, such as Mike and Joe Dundee, used the name.

It was often the way to take a name with a reputation for winning. Most of those who read this book will remember the former heavyweight champion Jersey Joe Walcott, but few realize he took his name from Joe Walcott, a former welterweight champion who was one of the great black fighters of earlier times.

There was not much money to be made fighting in small towns, but any money was good money to me in those rough years.

Somewhere in those months I read for the first time *A Frontier Doctor* by Henry F. Hoyt, a man who knew Billy the Kid and a number of the wild ones from the Texas–New Mexico border country. Another excellent book is *The Look of the West in 1860* by Sir Richard Burton, the Englishman who explored the upper reaches of the Nile and translated the *Arabian Nights*. I valued his work because he was an outsider who had traveled much on frontiers and was a keen observer.

A very valuable collection, which I did not come upon until much later, is *Pioneers of the San Juan*, the stories of people from the southwest corner of Colorado as collected by the D.A.R. (Daughters of the American Revolution). These are on-the-spot recollections of pioneers, and an important piece of work for which they must be much commended.

Six Years with the Texas Rangers by James Gillette and the *Reminiscences of a Ranchman* by Edgar Beecher Bronson were also valuable books I read during this time.

To list all the books that contributed to my education would be impossible, but the few mentioned will illustrate some of the trends. Yet I had no desire to be confined, and my interests led in all directions. My problem was that, having no home as such, I could not accumulate books, and many of those I most wanted simply were not to be found in public libraries (which must bend to the wishes of the greatest number). It was not until I married that I began to gather the working library I now possess.

My library is not simply an accumulation of books. Each book has its reason for being there, and there is no deadwood on those shelves. Those I have are what I believe to be the best in their field, and if not that, they at least have something of value to offer. I have no book I could not read again with profit, and most of them require re-reading. Occasionally, when not too pressed to get on with a story, I will go along the shelves, take down a half-dozen books, and just browse through them.

In my books, men long dead, such as Aristotle, Maimonides, Josephus, and Ibn Khaldun, offer their thoughts freely; one can visit India with Megasthenes or al-Biruni, China with Ibn Batuta, and the Holy Land with Ibn Jubayr. I can study the architecture of castles, cathedrals, mosques, and pyramids.

When very young, I attended a Bible school conducted by a man who knew his subject well. Later, I read the Bible several times, as well as the writings of Josephus, who lived shortly after the time of Jesus. It is a period on which we have many books aside from the Bible, and much on the Roman history of the time. I have read the Koran as well and find it has much to offer.

Shortly before World War II, I was invited to attend a lecture at the University of Oklahoma. Two quite gifted speakers were each to talk for a few minutes, and the feature of the evening was to be an address by George Milburn.

An Oklahoman who had made a name for himself in the short story field, Milburn had had stories published by H. L. Mencken's *American Mercury*, *Harper's*, and others. He was a gifted writer. But George was a writer, not a speaker, and this was his first time as the latter. Obviously he had written a good speech, but he just could not put it together. He stumbled and floundered and we all suffered with him. Finally, he seemed to get started, and then a train whistle blew somewhere outside and it might as well have cut his throat.

All present were in sympathy with him, but sitting there I suffered as much as he did, I believe, for I could see myself in the same position. At the time I did not have the courage to stand up and say my name in public. What I had seen happen to George Milburn could happen to me, and because I was confident that I was going to "make it," I knew it would happen.

What to do? I knew I would never attend a class, as I would avoid even trying to speak, so I decided the thing to do was to take the bull by the horns and just start speaking. I let the word get around that I was open for speaking engagements, knowing that sooner or later I would be challenged and have to make good. I was hoping it would happen in a small town where nobody knew me. It came about in just that way.

The night before the speech I did not sleep. The day of the lecture I decided I could not go through with it. A lady was driving some distance to pick me up and I called her to beg off. It was too late. She was already on her way.

All I wanted now was to get out of it, any way I could. I was sure I would make an unholy fool of myself trying to speak to any sort of a crowd, yet I could think of no way out. And then she arrived. With a dreadful sinking feeling, as of a man going to his execution, I got in the car and we turned to leave. I thought of jumping out. I thought of everything. We were rolling down the highway then and I was making small talk, trying to think of some way out.

There was no way. I had gotten myself into this fix and must see it through. On stage I reached into my pocket for my notes and they were not there. As surely as I began to search my pockets for them, somebody would snicker and I would have had it. So I began to talk without them, and somehow the evening passed and everybody seemed pleased. Especially me, as I was off the hook.

That was a beginning, and many years ago, but I firmly believe that if *I* could become a speaker, anybody can do anything if he or she wants to enough. Since that time I have appeared on the platform with a former President of the United States, a Supreme Court Justice, and many others. Education takes many forms and this was an important part of my education. Of course, if one is to speak, one must have something worth saying, and say it intelligently. The important lesson to be learned is that one's principal enemy in such cases is oneself.

A thing to remember is that the audience wants you to be good. No matter whether they know you or not, they do not want to be bored, so whether you realize it or not, they are pulling for you.

This is an age of communication. At one time or another, nearly everyone will have to stand up and sell his bill of goods, whatever it may be.

All young men and women owe it to themselves to be able to write a letter on not more than one page, to set forth an idea or possible plan. That same young person should, in a few brief spoken words, be able to deliver that idea orally.

No need for details, for if the idea is expressed

well, there will be questions, and the details can come later.

That day back in Oklahoma when I decided to become a public speaker was one of the most important in my life.

22

An interesting aspect of our history is the fascination that court trials held for the American citizen, not only in the West but elsewhere as well. In those days of few theaters some of the best drama was offered in courtrooms, and on the days when courts were busy the citizens drove or rode into town, crowding the streets and the plazas, eager for a seat in a courtroom to watch the trials.

The attorneys, fully aware of their importance, held center stage, and each had his supporters and following. Each was aware that his arguments would be discussed pro and con for months, and each savored quotations from the Bible, Shakespeare, and the classics, preparing every oration with care.

Many attorneys were great extemporaneous speakers, playing to the galleries as well as to the jury. Most citizens knew something of law, understanding a good bit about land titles, water rights, bills of sale, and other legal agreements necessary to their existence. However, they usually knew a good bit more than the average citizen today, because they attended such trials and listened to and discussed the questions before the court.

Blackstone was the key to much western law and in some areas the only law book known. Most lawyers had studied Blackstone, *Greenleaf's On Evidence*, and much else that was available. Usually they learned their law in the office of a known attorney, serving as clerks until ready to take the bar exam and go out on their own.

Naturally, as I was writing about early America, I read a good bit of Blackstone, two histories of American law, as well as John Reeves's *History of English Law* in four volumes, and Frank Kent's *Commentaries* in another four volumes. The development of law in many countries had always been of interest to me and I studied to a limited degree the history of the laws of the Lombards and of Justinian's code, as well as *Crime and Punishment in Mogul India* and *Crime and the Courts in England, 1660–1800* by Beattie.

Although some of what I was learning might someday be of use, I was not studying for that purpose, but, again, simply because I wished to know. My father had a considerable knowledge of law and was himself an interested follower of several attorneys who were friends. Their cases were often discussed at home, so all of us developed an interest in the law.

After that first lecture, I spoke as often as possible, at schools, colleges, county libraries, and the Farmer's Union, simply because I wanted to get better at it and because I knew a time would come when it would be important to me to speak well. It was another aspect of my education, and one of the most important. Again, as with writing, one never knows enough and one is never good enough.

I was never without a book, carrying one with me wherever I went and reading at every opportunity. Often I would eat alone in restaurants, arriving after the rush period and spending a good bit of time over coffee, reading, taking notes on books I expected to write, or thinking about what I was reading.

We are fortunate that we have so many excellent books available, on almost any subject that can be imagined, including many fine books on our own times and what to make of them. Yet there is also a tendency of late for some of our writers to become nit-pickers, looking not for ability in men and women, but for scandal. There is no great man in history who could have withstood the sort of journalism that focuses closely on issues of gossip.

What we really want to know is, does he have the ability? Does he have the knowledge? Have his past actions given us reason to believe he can lead? Has he had executive experience?

Unthinking people often despise politicians, but if we do not have the best people in politics, it is our own fault. Politics is the art of making civilization work.

Many young people despise compromise, but without it, the world would come to a standstill. If I cannot have my way and you cannot have yours, perhaps there is a middle ground we can both accept. It is as simple as that, and every day of our lives we are compromising in every possible way, adjusting and adapting to what needs to be done.

If one is not well informed on what is happening in our world today, an individual can only blame him or herself, for information is available everywhere. Bias can and does slip through, so one should not listen exclusively to one television news source or read the editorials of but one newspaper.

To make democracy work, we must be a nation of participants, not simply observers. One who does not vote has no right to complain.

The old civilizations in the new world continued to fascinate me. Early on, I had written several articles on the subject which were published. I had also done a short piece on Simon Bolívar, one of the great liberators of Latin America, as well as a piece on Henri Christophe, "The Black King of Haiti," and had visited his Citadel, where he prepared to defend his island against the French in an attack that never came.

I continued to read, working my way through most of what Hemingway had written up to that time, and finding his short stories better than his novels. I had known people like those in *The Sun Also Rises* and had not found them interesting, just a bunch of self-involved people who were coming from nowhere and for the most part going nowhere.

His "Fifty Grand," based loosely on the long fistic feud between Jack Britton and Ted (Kid) Lewis is, I think, one of the best fight stories ever written. Jack London's "The Mexican" is another.

Hemingway obviously knew something of the series of fights that Lewis, a Jew from Whitechapel, London, had with Britton, an Irish-American. Both were welterweight champions at times, and altogether they fought each other twenty-two times, with the decision going first one way and then the other but with Britton winning most of them. The two men came to hate each other, an uncommon thing among fighters, who rarely have any more feeling about the other fighter than do opposing basketball players or golfers.

I have never worked with anyone on a story and have never wanted to, nor has anyone ever done any research for me. The research is half the fun of writing, and delving into old books and records turns up so many unexpected treasures. The creation of a story is something I have never wished to share, and I am not even sure that I could function well working with someone else, as creativity to me is such an individual matter.

Writing can be fun, and so it has been for me. Once I was established to the point that editors were asking me for stories, I found I could explore in many directions just so far as I did not forget what people wished to read. Writing *The Walking Drum* was pure pleasure. With that book I had the chance to move into another era and re-create what was happening then with a sense of real participation.

The Arab boy whose comments started me thinking about the settlement of Asia was mistaken. Or perhaps he was speaking of his family and no others, but when I began researching the subject, I discovered that Arab seafaring people had been in Indonesian waters not four hundred years earlier but fully one thousand years before that day off the coast of Borneo.

We do not know when the exploration of what is now Indonesia began, but we do know that at a small village called Muara Kaman, some hundred miles inland from the coast of Borneo on the Mahakam River, several inscriptions have been found that date from A.D. 400.

We know that a Hindu culture existed there for a time, and that a lively trade developed with both India and China. The Tamils of southern India, always great mariners, traded with the Indonesian peoples as well as those of Madagascar off the coast of Africa. At a time when, so far as we know, only Phoenicians had sailed the Atlantic coasts, Tamils were already making voyages across two thousand miles of open sea.

Our Western culture is unbelievably rich, yet without a doubt one of the great civilizing factors in the Far East was the diffusion of ideas between India and China, and eventually, Japan and Korea.

I-Tsing made a pilgrimage to India and the islands to study Buddhism between A.D. 671 and

692, surviving some dangerous days at sea in small ships. At the time there were at least two kingdoms in Sumatra; the largest, Shrivijaya, eventually triumphed over the other and became something of a naval power in the area. Its capital was at Palembang, still an interesting, attractive city. At about this time or a bit later that massive monument to Mahayana Buddhism, the Barabudur, was built on an inland plateau in Java which is visited each year by many travelers.

Atisa, a monk from Tibet, studied in Shrivijaya for some time, and wrote of it. It had become over the years something of a focal point for Buddhist learning, with pilgrims coming from India and China as well as many other areas where Buddhism had taken hold. Many scholars sought instruction there.

The first positive date for China's knowledge of Bali is 977, but sometime before that one of the kings of Sumatra established an institution at Nalanda, the greatest center of Buddhist learning in India, and undoubtedly one of the greatest educational institutions in the world's history, where scholars from all Asia gathered to study.

Living as we do in the present, we do not realize that there is no present, only a shifting scene that is not two days the same, and that all we know today may be and will be gone tomorrow. On that day in Singapore where I began this book, Singapore was a faraway, remote place, to which few people traveled and which many could not locate on a globe. Now planes fly there constantly and your next-door neighbor has probably vacationed there.

This dramatic change began, of course, with World War II. On the U.S.S. *Boise* returning from France, I sat entranced listening to a farm boy from Iowa telling of his experiences in Burma and India, while another talked of New Guinea and Australia. Not too many years before, I talked little about my travels because I simply was not believed. Now, in the space of a few years, all had changed.

In that space of time an entire generation of Americans had spread over the world to a degree previously impossible. Tourist and commercial travel have followed, but unfortunately too little is known by most travelers for them to understand what they are seeing, or that they are often looking upon a vanished greatness that is now rising again.

The world with which we are now familiar will have largely disappeared within twenty years, probably fewer. Business machines are changing the face of the world, and the work force demands greater skills than ever before. When I started my knockabout years, there was much a man could do who was simply strong. That is no longer true. Those young people of whatever race or nationality who loiter along streets or gather in gangs are going nowhere without education and training, but education is there for them now, as it was for me. Fortunately, I was born into a family of readers and knew where to go. These other youths now must look, must find their own way, and it is never easy. The fact remains that it can be done, now as well as then. All that is needed is the will, and the idea.

And then the long days and nights of reading, thinking, learning. One has to remember the old Chinese adage, "A journey of a thousand miles begins with a single step." One just has to keep taking that step over and over again. There is no easy way; there are no shortcuts.

Yet I have taken those steps and am still taking them.

In my research I found that secondary sources were often interesting, but I preferred whenever possible to go to the originals, such as *The Periplus of the Outer Sea* by Marcian of Heracles, and later the *Periplus of the Erythraean Sea*, which is a guide to sailing and the market towns of the Indian Ocean and neighboring waters — a truly excellent book and one essential for much of what I was planning. The author is unknown but he was undoubtedly a merchant mariner or venturer in the years shortly after the time of Christ.

Parthian Stations by Isidore of Charax, and the *Periplus of Hanno*, I also read at about this time. I had long been fascinated by ancient seafaring, which was much more extensive than is generally believed. The *Chau Ju-Kua*, a book on seaports and markets of the Far East in the twelfth and thirteenth centuries (as translated by Hirth and Rockhill, both noted scholars in their field), is another valuable source.

Ancient Geography of India by Sir Alexander Cunningham is an excellent study in a field where not too much is available, as is *The History of Central Asia* by Rahula Sankrityayana. These were only a few of the many studies I discovered on areas in which I was interested, but all were valuable as well as exciting, interesting reading. Gradually, as I read, the world of ancient and medieval Asia began to take shape for me. From the beginning I had been fascinated by the peoples who migrated out of Central Asia into Europe or India. Many of our own ancestral roots lie deep in those vast steppes and grasslands, which seemed to produce an unlimited supply of fierce Scythian or related warriors.

It was interesting, too, that India, many times invaded, never invaded anyone. They had all they wanted and no need to leave their country for anything. Some of those who did invade, such as Alexander the Great and Mahmud of Ghazni, were simply seeking new worlds to conquer or to advance the Faith. Other peoples who moved into India did so to escape population pressures elsewhere, such as the Sakas, who settled in Nepal — and one of whose ancestors was Buddha.

Associate with the noblest people you can find; read the best books; live with the mighty. But learn to be happy alone.

Rely upon your own energies, and so not wait for, or depend on other people.

— PROFESSOR THOMAS DAVIDSON

23

Studies have been done on the functioning of the brain, and scientists have somewhat nervously approached the question of mind. Up to now, too little attention has been given to the mind, how it functions or can be made to function.

There has been much discussion of creativity, often considered a rare gift, although by some a condition bordering on insanity. Certain people have enjoyed searching out those artists and writers with other problems and pointing to them as illustrations. To do this they must turn away from many quietly normal human beings who create enormously and have no more than the usual collection of human follies and foibles.

Personally, I do not believe the human mind has any limits but those we impose ourselves.

I believe that creativity and inventiveness are there for anybody willing to apply himself. I do not believe that man has even begun to realize who he is or what he can become. So far he has been playing it by ear, following paths of least resistance, getting by — because most others were just getting by too.

I believe that man has been living and is living in a Neanderthal state of mind. Mentally, we are still flaking rocks for scraping stones or chipping them for arrowheads. The life that lies before us will no longer permit such wastefulness or neglect. We are moving into outer space, where the problems will be infinitely greater and will demand quicker, more accurate solutions. We cannot trust our destinies to machines alone. Man must make his own decisions.

We simply must free the mind from its fetters and permit it to function without restraint. Many of us have learned to supply ourselves with the raw materials and then allow the subconscious to take over. This is what creativity is. One must condition oneself for the process and then let it proceed.

We all are possessed of knowledge we do not realize we have. This is the accumulation over the years of our subconscious recognitions and appreciations. The information lies there awaiting use, not understood, because we make no demands upon it — although every once in a while a bright idea appears or some unexpected solution to a problem becomes evident.

We must formulate a process for using the subconscious on demand, a simple matter of conditioning. We must learn to pose our problems, supply materials, and let it happen. A writer, or for that matter any artist, is continually making demands upon the subconscious and producing results. The process is there for anyone; it only demands that we make the effort, and by study arrive at the best methods for doing so. It is rather amazing that we spend millions developing transistors and chips that can do only what man can already do within himself. Of course, the transistors and chips can do much work that men need not do, saving enormous amounts of time and energy, but the answer lies within man himself.

A wanderer I had been through most of my early years, and now that I had my own home, my wandering continued, but among books. No longer could I find most of the books I wanted in libraries. I had to seek them out in foreign or secondhand-book stores, which was a pleasure in itself. When seeking books, one always comes upon unexpected treasures or books on subjects that one has never heard of, or heard mentioned only in passing.

Now I knew what I wished to learn and could direct my education with more intelligence.

Slowly I began to place on my shelves the books I wanted. When the shelves were first installed, one workman doubted they would ever be filled, yet a few years later they were crammed with books, filling every available niche.

These were not nice even rows of books in similar bindings but often were battered old veterans moving from the hands of one lover to another, valued for their contents and nothing else. Understand me: I love well-bound books and have many. I love the feel of them, the texture of their bindings and paper, everything about them, but many very excellent books have gone out of print, no longer in sufficient demand to warrant republishing.

Often these are the books I want most and the only place to find many of them is when some collector dies and his library is sold.

I have made no effort to gather the so-called great books. Most of them I read during my knock-about years. The books I have are of immediate as well as lasting interest, and already my library has grown beyond the space available. A book that stands on my shelf may well be the result of reading a dozen or twenty books or, at least, examining them, for I have tried to get the best.

If you come looking for old friends you will find a few. *Candide*, *A Sentimental Journey*, *The Brothers Karamazov*, Byron's *Childe Harold*, much of Tennyson, but many of the books will be strangers. There will be books on the food that people ate and how they ate it, on their costumes, their homes, and how they entertained themselves. History to me is the story of people and how they lived, not just an endless story of dynasties and wars. They are a part of the story, of course, and my library is very complete on how wars were conducted, castles built and defended, armies supplied, and treaties arrived at.

The beauty of educating oneself as I was doing, or as anyone can do, is that there are no limits to what can be learned. All that is learned demands contemplation, and so one is never at a loss for something to do.

When writing of Chinese literature earlier, a

book I failed to mention was the *Chin P'ing Mei* by Hsu Wei. This is a somewhat pornographic novel written of Hsi Men and his six wives, written at about the time of Shakespeare.

Meeting the censor on the street, the author was asked what he was writing, and was told that the censor wished to see it immediately upon its completion. At the time China was going through one of its periods of strict censorship, so Hsu Wei, according to the story, made plans.

He had his book printed on extremely thin rice paper and before submitting it to the censor he carefully planted a small dab of poison on the upper right-hand corner of each page.

24

Although involved with studying the Far East, I at no time neglected my study of the American West. Much of what I was writing concerned the West and it was my duty as a writer to present as honest a portrayal as possible. To that end I was not only traveling the country but reading approximately thirty books a year on the West in its many aspects.

For example, I read *Ancient Hunters of the Far West* by Malcolm Rogers, *Journey to the Rocky Mountains, 1839* by Fred A. Wizlenzenus, *Humboldt to the Pacific* by Jacob H. Schiel, *Conquest of New Mexico and California 1846–48* by Philip St. George Cooke, *A History of New Mexico* by Gaspar Perez de Villagra, *New England Indians*, Volumes I and II, by Leo Bonfanti, and many more.

Along with these, I read *The History of Ideas* by George Boas, *Journal of a Novel* by John Steinbeck (which he kept while writing *East of Eden*), and the *The Natural Geography of Plants* by Henry A. Gleason and Arthur Cronquist.

This is a fair sampling, but no more than that. Most of this time I was crisscrossing the country with my family, visiting lonely water holes, old line-camps, cliff dwellings, and the places where frontier history happened. Wherever possible, I took along some old cowboy or miner who would tell me who had lived where and who had worked the claims. Along with such information, there were always a lot of stories, glimpses of personalities, of bad horses, of bronc riders and Indians.

Prowling about in the mountains was always exciting, discovering areas I would someday use in a story or some bit of information that would add to another. As I was writing one story, I was always preparing for others, and loving every moment of it.

People often ask me if I ride horseback. To tell you the truth, I have not been on a horse in years. Yet there is no reason why one should ride a horse to write about it, and I did my riding in the past. Now I ride to the sites I wish to explore in a four-wheel-drive vehicle and then get out and hike.

Why? Because I am constantly looking for artifacts, for plants I wish to identify, for others whose manner of growth I wish to understand. To do this, it is better to be on foot. There are crevasses I wish to crawl into, ruins I wish to check out, and many such things.

If one of my characters is wounded, I want him to treat his wounds with what he would find available. Most western men were familiar with simple home remedies as well as some Indian treatments. Few people had ready access to a doctor, even in the eastern states, and the doctors themselves often used home remedies they had inherited from older physicians. One did the best one could with what one had, so in my stories the treatments used are what would be available at the time and place.

In the earliest days in the mountains, infection was rare. In the fresh mountain air and on the diet available, men recovered rapidly from serious wounds. Some of the Indian remedies were quite useful, but as we all know, many people simply recover. The mountain men, for example, and western men generally, were in excellent health to begin with.

Few carried even a pound of excess weight. Most were constantly moving, walking, running, bending, kneeling to set a trap, actively exercising. Their drinking binges were rare, as whiskey was available only in towns, and such bouts with the bottle were often separated by months or even years.

To write well of the West, it is essential to have considerable basic knowledge, and to continue to learn.

Many of the buffalo hunters, for example, disliked the killing, but it was their way of making a living, and no matter what one thinks now, the buffalo had to go. On those vast plains where buffalo roamed (and where a buffalo wants to go, he goes!) there are now great universities, hospitals, homes, and food enough raised to feed half the world.

Shortly after World War II, when I was living in Los Angeles, I often took the train or bus to one of the towns near the Grand Canyon. Several times it was Peach Springs, Arizona. I knew no one there but would get off the bus and backpack into the canyons branching off from the Grand Canyon and spend three or four days hiking wild country, alone.

Most of my friends or acquaintances had jobs from which they could not get away, and not many of them would accept the rugged conditions I took for granted. Another place I often went was the wilderness area of Sycamore Canyon in Arizona. In those days there was a small railroad — the Verde-Mix, I believe it was called — and for a couple of dollars one could buy a ticket and the train crew would drop you off and pick you up later. Several times I went up into the Sycamore Canyon area, exploring, camping, simply living the life.

It is a beautiful area, near Oak Creek Canyon and Sedona, but kept even now as a wilderness, as well it should be.

We are fortunate indeed to have the works of many enlightened, interested travelers in the West at its various stages. For my purposes, the West was any place beyond the existing frontier, which at first was east of the Appalachians. We have such works, for example, as *Travels Through the Middle Settlements of North America, 1759–1760* by Reverend Andrew Burnaby, *Travels in America 1798–1802* by John Davis, *Early Travels in Tennessee* by Samuel Cole Williams, and many others, including John Bradbury's *Travels in the Interior of*

America in the Years 1809, 1810, and 1811. In this latter case we were indeed fortunate, as Bradbury was a naturalist and was on the spot when the New Madrid earthquake happened, the most devastating quake to strike North America in historic times. The quake occurred in Missouri and the neighboring areas, created Reelfoot Lake in Tennessee, and was felt as far away as Boston, Massachusetts, and Charleston, South Carolina.

The West of which so much is written did not suddenly happen. It was built upon much that had gone before. The travel accounts mentioned earlier were through country where the stage was being set for a different kind of life.

I must add that some of the Englishmen traveling in the West were much offended that men did not spring to attend to their horses upon their arrival at an inn. There were usually men hanging about, but they were living in a country where men did for themselves, and not as in Britain or France, where someone was always ready to serve. The independence of the frontiersman offended some travelers, but the frontiersman had no reason to be obsequious. There were no class lines, and a man was what he made himself to be. If the tavern in question had no one on hand to take one's horse, he stabled and fed it himself.

We are fortunate as well that there were so many travelers who not only wandered the country but wrote excellent accounts of what they saw, so we can know what it was like at almost any point in time.

My own family history was often a reference point for me. I have not written about it thus far, but it was useful in calculating the generations of other families. On one side of my family (and probably at least three) I am a tenth-generation American, and I have used my own family as a measuring stick for others of whom I write.

Always, my reading was to understand, and it was for background. To re-create the life of a period in fiction, one must know as much as possible. What were the roads and trails like? How were taverns kept? What food might be available to a traveler? What about homes at various financial levels? And clothing? What did a pistol cost? Or ammunition?

If I knew how others were living, I would know how my characters had to live.

In checking out terrain, I often spent time just sitting and looking, or possibly hiking the trails to get an estimate of the time required.

How long would it take an able-bodied, reasonably athletic man to cross such a mountain? How long if he was injured in some way? Where could he find some primitive shelter if need be?

Many of the places about which I write were places I encountered during my knockabout years, where I worked, passed through, or camped. Others were simply places I passed by and noticed, or of which I learned from some chap in a café.

By the time I married, all that was behind me, but much of the traveling I did with my family was important. By that time I had learned to focus on what was most essential and I was seeking out particular places or people.

In Colorado we visited Mesa Verde and its Anasazi ruins again and again, learning a little more each time. At least twice we were present at an Illuminaria, where the rooms of Cliff Palace were lighted at night by candles.

We arrived shortly before dark and were in place before the candles were lighted. We had with us our friend Charlie Daniels, the country-western singer, and Cliff Brycelea, the Navajo artist whose painting is featured on the cover of my book *The Haunted Mesa*. Cliff commented that what we were seeing must have been much what it was like when inhabited. From down the canyon came eerie music — bagpipes, I believe — but far enough away to provide a sense of added weirdness to the scene.

As the candles burned down, those of us who had brought flashlights helped to guide others over the narrow trails and up steep stairways. I believe if the ghosts of the Anasazi linger among those dwellings, they would have been pleased to see them lighted once again. It was a hauntingly beautiful sight that remains with me still.

During the years that followed, I went often to visit cliff dwellings or other Anasazi ruins. I came to see, to learn, and to disturb nothing. Let the archaeologists who know what they are doing handle that. A pot or a broken fragment removed from its discovery site has lost much of its value. Slowly, with a discovery here and one there, the history of the Southwest is put together, but it is painstaking work, and the pot someone carries away to keep or to sell may be the key piece that would reveal much to the trained eye. Once on someone's shelf and away from where it was found, the piece has lost most of its value.

Long ago, I had hiked up the floor of Mancos Canyon. Now I wished to stand at about the middle and get an overlook from the rim. With my family and an archaeologist who was working for the Utes on their reservation, we started to drive out to the rim and were overtaken by a police car.

Did we have a permit? We did not. Frank, the archaeologist, identified himself. The Ute police officer was cool. "I know who you are, and" — he indicated me — "I know who he is. I read his books. But if you don't have a permit, you can't go."

We did not attempt to argue the case. This was their reservation, their home, and we obeyed the rules. He followed us back to headquarters to make sure we did.

A short time later, accompanied by three archaeologists and a Ute Indian, my family and I spent a night in a cliff dwelling on the Ute Reservation. The archaeologists arranged the affair and we drove out in four-wheel-drive vehicles to arrive just before sundown.

The cliff dwelling was in a deep canyon filled with trees, some of which had been lightning-struck. It was in a remote area and we climbed down into the canyon to find our places. There had been no cleanup there. The place was as time had left it: a few scattered human bones, some of the tiny corncobs, a few shards of broken pottery.

Kathy and I chose a *kiva* (ceremonial center) in which to spread our sleeping bags, and shortly after we arrived, there was a thunderstorm.

Nature seemed to have deliberately planned our entertainment, for there was rolling thunder, unusually loud because of the narrow canyon, and many flashes of brilliant lightning, but only a few scattered drops of rain fell. Nature put on a grand show for upward of an hour. Then the sky cleared, the moon came out, and we had a truly magnificent night.

Art Cuthair, the Ute who was with us, may well have been the first Indian to spend a night in a cliff dwelling since the Anasazi abandoned them. Many Indians are uncomfortable at disturbing the spirits of the former inhabitants.

(Art has been involved in stabilizing some ruins and in laying out trails for the guided tours the Utes give for visitors wishing to see the dwellings as they were found.)

We settled in for the night, each in his or her own way. I was determined to remain awake and enjoy every moment of the experience to the utmost.

Often we heard eerie sounds, whisperings and movements. The wind? The leaves? Small animals or birds? Or something else? Something from the past, perhaps, something from the forgotten years?

The moon was bright, and soon coyotes were singing their plaintive songs. Other Indians had stopped by to see us but would not stay the night. They went to sleep out of the canyon, away from the cliff houses.

Some of us slept; some remained awake with me. None of us talked. It was a time for listening. Once, faint and far-off, there seemed to be the sound of a flute or some wind instrument.

It is sometimes said that few archaeologists have ever spent a night in a cliff dwelling, and that no archaeologist has spent two nights.

However, I regretted the coming of day, although ready enough for breakfast.

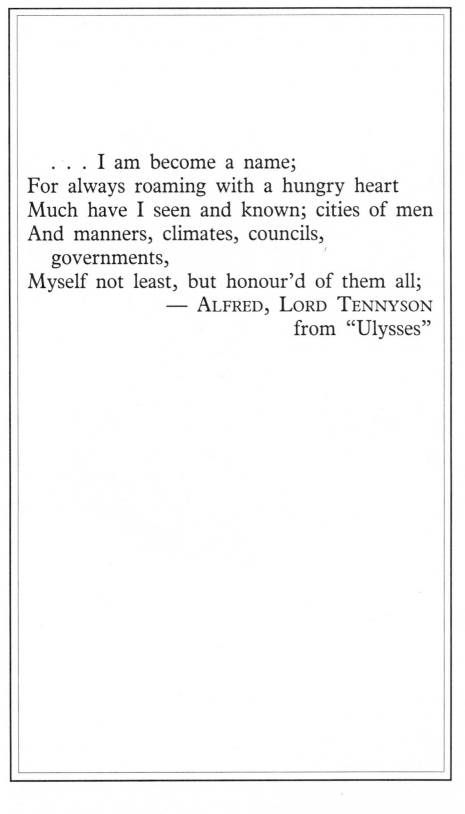

. . . I am become a name;
For always roaming with a hungry heart
Much have I seen and known; cities of men
And manners, climates, councils,
    governments,
Myself not least, but honour'd of them all;
                    — ALFRED, LORD TENNYSON
                        from "Ulysses"

25

My study of Africa began some years ago when I wrote a review for Carter G. Woodson's *The African Background Outlined*. Shortly after that, I reviewed *Black Folk: Then and Now* by W.E.B. Du Bois. Until then, my knowledge of Africa largely stemmed from adventure stories or Burton's books on Central Africa when he was searching for the sources of the Nile, although back in my Jamestown days, I had read Stanley's search for Dr. Livingstone, called *How I Found Livingstone*, as well as its sequel, *Through the Dark Continent*.

Of North Africa, the Sahara Desert, Libya, Morocco, and Algiers, I knew quite a bit. Those areas were largely inhabited by Berbers, a white people, and by Arabs — the two often lumped together simply as Moors.

Long ago, Greeks had settled along the coast and later the Phoenicians had established themselves at Carthage, to become a dominant power until destroyed by Rome. The influence of all these peoples was felt along both the Mediterranean and Atlantic coasts of Africa.

My first knowledge of the great black empires of the Niger region had come from reading the travels of Ibn Battutah, however, so when I first came upon Woodson's book, I was prepared for what he had to say, regretting the limited space in which he had to say it.

In the following years I read nearly two dozen books on some phase of Africa and its history, finding many that merely scratched the surface.

Later, when time permitted, I returned to Africa in *Travels in Ethiopia* by David Buxton, *The Mountains of Rasseles* by Thomas Pakenham, *A Short History of South Africa* by Leopold Marquard, *South Africa* by Brian Fagan, *The Ancient Kingdoms of the Nile* by Walter Fairservis, and that gem *The Search For the Tassili Frescoes* by Henry Lhote.

During the time I worked in mines, I had been fortunate to meet a number of old miners who had worked in Virginia City, Nevada, during its boom days and after. At the Katherine Mine it was the custom, as in others as well, for the miners to gather at the station to await the cage that would take them to the top when the shift was over. There they would wait and listen for their shots to go off from the fuses lighted before coming out. It was imperative to count the shots and be sure all the holes fired; otherwise one might, the following morning, drill into a missed hole, detonating the unexploded powder. This could mean death or serious injury to the miner and anyone close by.

During this time of sitting around the station, stories would be told, and I learned much that later served well in creating the background for my book *Comstock Lode.*

Virginia City in its heyday was certainly one of the most remarkable of the many remarkable boom camps that flared to brief glory in the West and then settled down to the day-to-day job of getting the ore out. The so-called Comstock Lode was one of the richest mineral discoveries ever made and the life there was rich and colorful, creating several millionaires, one of whom was John Mackay.

John Mackay walked into Virginia City broke and when he left he was worth $200 million. He made it through a shrewd appreciation of the lay of the land, the probabilities of what must have happened when the great rift was created that was the source of the silver, followed by quiet purchase of seemingly played-out claims.

John Mackay not only made his millions in Virginia City, he knew how to spend them, and when Jay Gould's transatlantic cable system charged him too much for cables to his wife, Mackay built his own cable.

There was much written material available on Virginia City and the mines, but the miners I had met talked of the personalities of those involved, so their names and quality were generally known to me before I began my study. This, again, was a product of simply listening. Young men are inclined to be full of themselves — their desires, goals, and ambitions — yet often they are talking when they should be listening, and I know that at times that included me.

My own work in the mines and doing assessment work on mining claims also helped to provide background. I had actually worked with a single-jack and hand drill, although during my time most mining was done with machines. On assessment work, no such machines were available and when we got into hard rock it was necessary to drill by hand. By the time I came along, the boom years in Virginia City were long gone, but many of the older miners had worked that period as young men. It had been an exciting time, and they forgot very little of it.

During my mining days I had participated in the last gold rush, if such it could be called, in the Rocky Mountain West. There were to be other discoveries, but this was the last boom, the last rush for claims. At the time I was employed at the Katherine Mine on the Colorado, and four of us took time off and drove to Weepah, Nevada, not far from Tonopah, another famous mining boom town.

The rush to Weepah was made largely by car — Fords, Chevys, and a car briefly popular, the Star. Others rode horseback or drove in buck-boards or wagons. By the time we arrived to stake our claims, much good land was gone but each of us found a spot, and I chanced on one that had been overlooked.

By the time my ground was staked, I had little confidence in Weepah as a "great discovery," so when a man came along with a fat roll of bills and no judgment I promptly sold my claim. I was the only one of the four of us who even made expenses on that trip. I sold out for $50, as I recall.

Down in the center of "town," there were the usual gamblers, several tents in which ladies were entertaining gentlemen, and several bars selling moonshine whiskey. The miners with whom I had made the rush were canny when it came to ore, and they were not pleased with what they saw, so after a few days we went back to work at the Katherine.

That was also the year, I believe, that I fought fire in the mining town of Chloride, Arizona, north of Kingman. We had come over, thinking of trying for a job at the Tennessee Mine, but the town caught fire and I found myself sloshing water over some very hot roofs. The water was passed up to me from below, and taken from barrels kept for the purpose along the streets. There weren't enough barrels and we lost a good fight. Also, if I am not mistaken, we lost a good miner, cowboy, and occasional street-fighter called One-Thumb Tom. A good man whom I did not know, he breathed fire into his lungs, or so I heard. In any such case, everybody helps, and we all tried. Unhappily, much of Chloride was burned on that day.

Often I am sad that our interests have turned away from the short story, for so many beautiful and great stories have been written and are now on the back shelf of the world's literature. The writing of a really fine short story is like the carving of a gem. I have written many but none of the quality to which I aspire. Over the years I have collected many which I have enjoyed, and still enjoy.

Looking back over my years of reading, I am amazed at how much really wonderful stuff there is out there, and it is a pity that anyone should deprive himself of the chance to read it, yet many do. Ours is not a leisurely time, and our readers prefer page-turners, stories or other books that lead one eagerly from page to page. It is also important, to those for whom reading is difficult, to have books that demand one read on, and on.

Yet many of the great books of the past were written for a more leisurely time, when people could sit and read by the fire, or comfortably in some great country house or cottage. Despite the fact that they were written for a different time and different audience, they have much to offer: great stories, brilliant characterizations, interesting ideas. Someone has said that one has no right to read the new books unless one has read the old. I do not agree, yet one should read the old books also.

Anatole France wrote, "A good critic is one who relates the adventures of his soul among masterpieces." Unfortunately we have too few of those today, and too little appreciation of just how much good writing there is out there.

It is a pity, too, that in the continuing process

of publishing books, so many of the old books have been lost to sight. I think, for example, of William Lecky's *History of European Morals* or, of a later vintage, Oswald Spengler's *The Decline of the West.* They are read, but by too few, and I haven't heard Lecky referred to but once or twice in many years.

Long ago I sat one day in a library where I had come upon the three volumes of E. A. Westermarck's *The History of Human Marriage.* Browsing through its pages, I kept chuckling and I know some other denizens of the library must have thought me off my rocker to be finding something at which to laugh in what was a dusty tome. Yet there is nothing more amusing than man and his customs, and in that case it was some studies of marriage by capture.

Knowing nothing, presumably, about gene pools, early men did still realize that intermarriage between relatives was not good, so when it came time for a young man to seek a wife, he would take with him one of the best fighters in his tribal group and set off to capture a bride. The other man, the "best man" of today's marriages, was to fight off the girl's relatives while he escaped with the bride.

In later years, when this was no longer necessary, it was often customary for the bride to suddenly leap on a horse and take off, pursued by the groom in a simulated "marriage by capture."

As I know of no case where the bride got away, I assume it was important that she choose a slow horse, or one she could control, while seeming to be trying to escape.

A cynic might say that one of man's civilizing attributes has been his convenient memory, which allows him to discover new reasons for old practices, or simply to forget their origin. This is true of some aspects of his religion as well as customs in regard to birth, coming of age, marriage, and death.

Knowledge is like money: To be of value it must circulate, and in circulating it can increase in quantity and, hopefully, in value.

Who remembers the millionaires of the past? Who even remembers the popular heroes? But we do remember a poor stonecutter in Athens named Socrates, a thief from the gutters of Paris named François Villon, an actor in London called Shakespeare, a poor farmer in Scotland named Robert Burns, and a weaver in Mayilapur who wrote the Kural.

Upon the shelves of our libraries, the world's greatest teachers await our questions.

Yet for those who have not been readers, my advice is to read what entertains you. Reading is fun. Reading is adventure. It is not important what you read at first, only that you read.

Many would advise the great books first, but often readers are not prepared for them. If you want to study the country from which you came, there are atlases with maps and there are good books on all countries, books of history, of travel, of current affairs.

Our libraries are not cloisters for an elite. They

are for the people, and if they are not used, the fault belongs to those who do not take advantage of their wealth. If one does not move on from what merely amuses to what interests, the fault lies in the reader, for everything is there.

My ranch has proved as necessary as my library, and so it is, in a sense — a living library, which can be studied at all seasons. I have added trees from other localities and shrubs as well, and study animal life of which there is a good bit: elk, deer, bear, mountain lion, badger, and much else. Old rail fences have been added, and when I describe them in a story they are just what is before my eyes. Every "improvement" on the place is actually a turn toward making it a more efficient site for what I have to do.

My ranch is important to me, because by wandering over its many acres, I have a chance to renew my feeling for the country, and despite the fact that I can write anywhere, I write best in the atmosphere of the kind of country about which I am writing.

Above all the ranch is a place where I can go to be alone. I have no visitors there, and want none. It is a place for work, and when I am on the place I am working. Yet mountains are mountains, and a mountain in India or Tibet looks very little different from a mountain in Colorado or Nevada. The plant growth is somewhat different, but I know about that, so there is no problem.

Walking in the early hours, one must walk with

care, for bears linger where the food is good. I often see where they have stripped a branch of chokecherries or serviceberries, or see mountain lion droppings often fresh from within the hour. It is a place where, in a matter of minutes, I can step from the log cabin where I live to the world of the last century.

Sometimes, with powerful glasses I keep at hand, I can see movement high on the ridge where bears are eating wild raspberries.

A couple of years ago I climbed that ridge, almost straight up through the forest at the end. It was a tough scramble, one I had not bargained for, but by the time I got where I wished to be, I was closer to the top than to the bottom and decided it would be easier to top out on the ridge than return the way I had come. I was wrong, but it did find me on a hillside matted with wild raspberries. As I always walk with a walkie-talkie, it was a simple matter to have myself picked up on the ridge, a private road built for four-wheel-drive vehicles.

Everything is grist for the mill, and someday that episode will find its place in a story.

26

Books are the building blocks of civilization, for without the written word, a man knows nothing beyond what occurs during his own brief years and, perhaps, in a few tales his parents tell him. Without books, we would never have known of Julius Caesar, Cleopatra, or Hannibal. George Washington would have been forgotten and Abraham Lincoln a vague memory.

When the Saxons landed in England and discovered Roman ruins, they believed them the work of giants. For without books there is no history; without books there would be no Greece, no Rome, no Babylon, and no Egypt. The pyramids would stand, and the Parthenon and many scattered ruins would slowly fall before the years. Not understanding what they were, man would make no effort to preserve them.

Without books we should very likely be a still-primitive people living in the shadow of traditions that faded with years until only a blur remained, and different memories would remember the past in different ways. A parent or a teacher has only his lifetime; a good book can teach forever.

Take, for example, your own family. How much do you know of who they were, how they lived, and what they thought three or four generations ago? Usually one knows something of his grandparents, perhaps his great-grandparents, but beyond that, all that remains are names, dates, and perhaps a few places. Unless something has been written, nothing is remembered and all our past becomes a cloudy dream pierced by few rays of light — old tax or military records, details of land transfers and the like, but nothing of who these people *were*.

We are rich in materials from the past, and what one book offers often dovetails with another until a clear historical pattern emerges. The pattern may not be entirely correct but one can work from it to find what is true or seems to be so. Fortunately we have maps that enable us to see the areas controlled by the various tribes or powers, the trade routes by land or sea, and the ports that accepted cargo from foreign vessels.

Traveling anywhere, I am invariably drawn to displays of books, often in old shops or simply used for display in some restaurant or hotel lobby. Rarely do I find interesting titles; most of those I do find were popular books of fifty to seventy years ago, some of them good reading even now. Nearly every western town antique shop has a few such books, and I cannot wait until I have examined them, as well as those in homes I visit. In one such store I found a copy of *The Goncourt Journals*, which I had recently read, and the *Shirley Letters* by Dame Shirley, in a later edition.

Once I was severely tempted to steal, and I have

often regretted that I did not yield to the temptation. I had gone to an old chateau on the outskirts of Paris to pick up an American girl with whom I had a date. She showed me a collection of eight or ten books of ancient maps, obviously bound by order of the owner, for they were from various places, on different grades of parchment, for example. I was utterly fascinated, for they represented a very real treasure. The former owner of the chateau had obviously known what he was doing and had assembled some very rare stuff. She told me the property had been inherited by a nephew who was selling it all as quickly as possible. As I was making a change of station the following day, there was no time for me to make any calls or try to formulate a deal, and I discovered later that the books had been sold as old paper. I can only hope someone recognized their value and rescued them. The latest date on any of the maps was 1475.

Such finds are rare, and I have never found any of those maps in the archives of the many libraries and collections I have haunted. I would have given much to own the maps and just as much for a few hours with the man who collected them, a man of knowledge and discrimination who knew what he wanted and had the patience to search them out.

Often, ambitious young men or women write, wanting to work for me or assist me in my research. What they do not understand is that it is a labor of love, and I would relinquish no part of it at any price. I do not need help; I need time.

I am jealous of these things. I want to read the books, examine the archives, trace the routes upon maps or charts. As I trace the routes I relive the lives; I walk with the caravans; I handle canvas on the ships; I pull an oar in the galleys. I know the smells of the sea because I have been there, and a thousand years ago they would have been no different. I know how it feels to ride a horse or a camel, and I want to live again with the caravans and the seafarers.

Each book I write is an adventure in itself. It is many adventures, into strange lands, strange places. It can be on the land of my own ranch, among the forests there, along the rugged ridges. Suddenly, as I weave the story, they are no longer just as I see them but are as they would have been one hundred, five hundred years earlier. They are places of enchantment, places where stories are born.

I am not some mill that grinds out stories simply to make a living. I am a man who loves to tell stories, who loves to share what he has seen and where history has been. I would like others to enjoy, as I have, the ancient towns and the old streets, the broken arches, the clock towers, the fallen walls where old smells linger, even after thousands of years.

I do not know if others feel as I do, nor do I care. I am a teller of stories with my own corner in the marketplace, and I speak of those long gone. In our country and elsewhere many men and women have added their dust to the earth and have been forgotten, but not by me. I have walked in their footsteps, seen the ruins of the houses they so carefully put together. I have seen their fingerprints in the clay, and sometimes in ancient caves I have seen a full hand-print on the wall, to show, perhaps, that they, too, had hands, that they, too, could shape the mortar of their lives into something more than it had been.

Beside every western trail lie buried the bodies of those who tried. In every western cemetery, Boot Hill or not, there are those who made it or almost did. I do not know their names, so I write my own stories and re-create their lives as I know they must have been. Briefly, they live again so their sons and grandsons can know how it was. I have never looked to critics for approval, only to those who knew, the men or women who can put a worn finger on a line and say, "That was how it was."

So much has been written of the individual that many have forgotten that our country was settled by families. The lone adventurer makes a good story, but the wagons west carried men, women, and children. The sod houses and the log cabins were lived in by families.

We writers, of course, stress the dramatic, and often readers forget the long periods of simply hard work that went to build the country. Gunfights were rare, raids by horse thieves rare, but hard work was every day. Fencing land, plowing land, grubbing roots for firewood, all this was every day.

Long dry stretches occurred, where everybody looked hopefully at a cloudless sky, praying for rain while the grass was eaten to stubble and the water holes dried out and cattle grew gaunt and a man saw his years of struggle going down, until some gave up and pulled out for that land of promise, farther west.

The West was a hard land with rarely enough rain, and when the rain did come it came too much at one time, in gully washers and flash floods. Many a farmer eked out a precarious living collecting bones of buffalo and other animals, as a wagonload of old bones would pay for a cartload of groceries. What other bones lay exposed on the plains we will never know, as all were gathered and disposed of in the same way.

The frontier was recognized at once as a fertile field for fiction. James Fenimore Cooper led off, followed by many others. Mayne Reid wrote *The Rifle Rangers*, *The Lost Rancho*, and *The Scalp Hunters* before 1883. James W. Steele had published his *Frontier Army Sketches* in 1872–73, Captain Charles King was writing, and Alfred Henry Lewis published his *Wolfville* stories in 1902, the same year Owen Wister's *The Virginian* appeared. In the meanwhile, several thousand dime novels had been circulated, touching upon all aspects of the West, real and unreal.

Eastern reporters had come west, returning with far-fetched stories or made-up interviews, quoting such people as Wild Bill Hickok with words he would never have spoken.

Western life was much more social than is realized by the average reader. Most western towns had bands made up of local citizens, and band concerts were frequent. Many frontier towns had baseball teams, often with imported pitchers. Footracing was a much bet-upon sport and it was not unknown for some gambler or group of gamblers to import a professional footracer from the East to match against some woodsman, cowboy, or Indian. Much money changed hands as a result of such races, and the Indians, being inveterate gamblers, often lost most of their ponies and tribal possessions. Horse racing was the biggest gamble of all, and the Indian was ever ready to come forward with a fast horse he wished to back. The Indians, who knew horses well, were often the winners in these races, never being as gullible as the white men assumed they were.

Churches or schools held "literaries," where visiting lecturers appeared or local citizens debated anything that came to mind. Bill Nye, the humorist, was a frequent visitor in many western towns, as was Mark Twain.

One of the amazing aspects of the frontier was the amount of classical research and writing that was going on. Quite often it was done by Army officers out of sheer boredom or pursuing interests of their own far from frontier guard duty or the pursuit of Indian war parties.

My educational efforts continued. I read *The Mississippi Valley Frontier* by John Anthony Caruso, *English Life in the Middle Ages* by Salzman, *A Union Soldier's Diary* by Albert W. Mosey, *The Natchez* by Antoine Simon Le Page du Pratz, *Alexander the Great and the Logistics of the Macedonian Army* by Donald W. Engels, and *My Life and Experiences Among Our Hostile Indians* by General O. O. Howard.

While traveling in France with my family, I had been reading *The Campaigns of Alexander* by Arrian. Alexander's problem of supply had intrigued me. I had some minor experience with feeding troops on the march, so it was an interesting question.

Moving large bodies of troops across country has to create enormous problems of supply, which would have to be well planned in advance. For Alexander, moving across vast stretches of Asia, the problems must have been critical, both for his men and his animals. His intelligence services had to be excellent, to keep him apprised of harvest and crop conditions, for he dare not risk thirty thousand men in an area where there had been crop failures or where there was no grass for his horses.

In the beginning his army was about that size, but it grew as he conquered new areas and absorbed bodies of troops from the conquered lands. Historians often take for granted the movements of armies and their logistical problems, but they were and continue to be critical.

Personally, I do not believe Alexander needed much persuasion to turn back. In conquering the

East he was being conquered by it, and for all his faults I believe he understood this. The core of his magnificent army was the Macedonians, and their strength had been watered down by troops of lesser quality. Moreover, before them lay some difficult and dangerous country where he could no longer rely on the information he was receiving. In fact, I should not be surprised if Alexander had himself encouraged the protests to give him an excuse to turn back.

The forces he had encountered were those of small kings, and the great powers of India lay before him.

Had he lived, he might have regrouped and returned, starting again with fresh troops added to his Macedonians, and better information than he possessed at that time.

He had yet to meet the Nanda kings, and the best of India's fighting men. Yet all this is speculation. Perhaps he had tired of conquest and wished to relax and enjoy what he had done.

One thing is certain: His legend still lives in those Asiatic mountains where the four worlds meet. After two thousand years, many are anxious to trace their ancestry to him or to his men. They take it for granted that his troops sired many children; some left their Legions and stayed behind. No other conqueror in history had that sort of impact to the same degree, for he created a legend and gave birth to a thousand stories. I think he would have liked that.

I am a part of all that I have met;
Yet all experience is an arch wherethro'
Gleams that untravell'd world, whose
   margin fades
For ever and for ever when I move.
How dull it is to pause, to make an end,
To rust unburnish'd, not to shine in use!
         — ALFRED, LORD TENNYSON
               from "Ulysses"

27

Knowledge — or perhaps in this instance the word *information* would be better — often comes in strange ways, but just as often in the commonplace passages of every day. It was in a bookstore in Belawan, a seaport of Medan in Sumatra that I first heard of the *Sejarah Melayu*, otherwise known as the *Malay Annals*.

The bookstore was small, with limited facilities, but had a curious cross-section of the flimsy popular magazines and the intellectual. I asked about a history of the area, and the clerk seemed either not to understand or did not wish to reveal his ignorance. But a very tall, very thin man with very black aquiline features mentioned the *Sejarah Melayu*. He also assured me it was difficult to obtain.

A few minutes of discussion led us to a coffeehouse, where we spent the afternoon. The young man was something of a scholar, a Moslem, but one of wide-ranging interests, and he was, as I was, lonely for talk of books, writers, and ideas.

He had attended school in India and later in Singapore, and now held some sort of government job in Sumatra, but he was a young man of ideas isolated from others of his kind. He spoke excellent English with a peculiar accent, and he explained about the *Sejarah Melayu.* It was a sort of history, he said, a book that had grown from a king list, probably by adding actual historical fact along with folk tales known of the various kings, maharajahs, sultans, and such, beginning with the installation of Seri Turi Buana, said to be a descendant of Alexander the Great, in 1179.

The procession of the king list and their stories leads finally to Sultan Abdul Rahman Shah in Lingga. He died in 1832 and was followed by his son Muhammad Shah, and the *Annals* ended with that name.

The area ruled by the various sultans covered most of the Malay Peninsula and the island of Sumatra. At the northern section of Sumatra was the kingdom of Atjeh, sometimes said to be a pirate kingdom somewhat like those in the Adriatic and adjoining waters in the days of the Roman republic.

The following day I had to return to my duties aboard ship, my brief leave over. There followed some hours of chipping rust, spotting it with red lead, and then repainting with the ship's colors. I managed to get ashore one more time, in the evening, and was taken to my friend's home, where he proudly showed me his small collection of European books. It was then I discovered that he read German and French as well as English.

We dined there quietly, with his family about, seemingly charmed and somewhat awed by their strange visitor. They all seemed cut from the same mold: slender, dark people with large, slow-moving eyes and gentle voices.

I never saw him again, but did leave with him some novels I had been given and had finished reading, among them *Lord Jim*, and *Hard Times* by Dickens.

A few years later I added to my library the C. C. Brown translation of the *Sejarah Melayu*. Although some stories date from an earlier time, it seems likely the book itself was written in 1612.

Being the sort of man I am and considering the life I have lived, it is not surprising that one of the intriguing aspects accompanying the exchange of ideas from culture to culture was the fact that most of the Buddhist pilgrims and teachers were also exponents of the martial arts. The basics of kung fu and karate came over the mountains from India or from the Buddhists of Khotan to China and Japan.

Bodhidharma, a master of the martial arts as well as a wanderer in search of knowledge and a teacher, brought his skills, after much travel, to the famed Shao Lin monastery. Bodhidharma was a disciple of one of India's greatest scholars, Nagarjuna, who originated the doctrine that became Ch'an in China and Zen in Japan. In his wanderings Bodhidharma became known in China as Ta-Mo; in Japan, as Daruma. He is often pictured as an old man with a twig over his shoulder from which a sandal is suspended.

Bodhidharma was the third son of an Indian king, probably a Pallava, and he was received at court by the Emperor Wu. Some reports have it that he lived long and finally passed away at the Shao Lin; others, that toward the end he left on the Silk Road toward the towns along the Kuenlun Mountains, perhaps to Khotan.

At no time in history of which I am aware was there such a diffusion of culture between two peoples as that between India and China in the Buddhist period. Pilgrims left China and made the long, fearful trek over the deserts and mountains to India, a journey that at the least took many months, but often years. Others went by sea in the vessels that were trading with India or the Persian Gulf ports. This was a journey of roughly two thousand miles over some of the roughest seas on earth, seas where piracy goes on, even today.

One of the first Buddhist scholars to reach China was Kumarajiva, who was residing in the Chinese capital as early as A.D. 401. By 412 he had translated more than one hundred Buddhist and other texts from Sanskrit into Chinese.

We know of dozens of monks who traveled to India and returned, as well as many missionaries from India to China, among them Dharmagupta. He is said to have written a book comprising minute geographical details of the many countries he visited, including details on their system of government, the food they ate, what they drank, wore, and studied. Unfortunately no copy seems to have survived of what would be an extremely valuable book.

A party of five monks started from China in

A.D. 399, led by Fa-hien. At Tun-hwang (the Caves of the Thousand Buddhas) the local official supplied them with all that was necessary to proceed but with dire warnings of what lay before them, which was the vast desert of the Taklamakan, roughly the size of Oklahoma and Texas combined. This desert is described by Fa-hien, speaking of the perils encountered: ". . . travellers who encounter them perish to a man. There is not a bird to be seen in the sky above, nor an animal of the ground below. Though you look all about to see where you can cross, you know not where to make your choice, the only mark and indication being the dry bones of the dead, scattered upon the sand."

It is the same today. Travelers find it necessary to grease their faces, as the skin becomes dry and cracks, causing bleeding sores. The oldest piece of paper in the world was found on the site of the ancient town of Lou-lan, paper dated (it could still be read) A.D. 130. (Paper is said to have been invented in China in 106.)

The desert is so dry that, in nearly two thousand years, that paper had not rotted away. On the site of Lou-lan, carved timbers have been found and even standing trees not far away, dead for centuries. Out in this desert there are ruins of vanished cities, perhaps of civilizations, all evidence of changing winds or perhaps of the uplifting of the Himalayas, cutting off the rains that once watered this desert.

Fa-hien did not return by the same route, but

317

embarked on a large vessel at Tamralipti. After fourteen days he reached Ceylon (Sri Lanka) where he remained to study for two years; then, boarding a Chinese merchant vessel, he began a voyage on which all aboard were close to death. He arrived back in China in 414 and began translating the works he had brought back with him. He died at the age of eighty-eight.

The T'ang dynasty, one of the most glorious in Chinese history, ruled in China from A.D. 618 to 907. Trade, travel, and cultural diffusion probably reached their highest peak during this period, when many Indians were living in China and many Chinese pilgrims were making the long treks to India.

Many books were translated from one language to the other, and although most were Buddhist, many concerned other aspects of culture, such as mathematics, astronomy, medicine, military tactics, and various aspects of government.

Nalanda University had become the most famous center of learning in Asia, with thousands of students coming from all parts of Asia to study, and many scholars in residence. Hiuen Tsang, perhaps the most distinguished of the many scholars, was born in A.D. 600 of a Confucian family. He became a Buddhist monk when only twenty and, by the age of twenty-nine, was en route to India. Discontented, as many in China were, with the books and teachings on Buddhism, he decided to go to the source and by the year 630 was studying in India. During the next fourteen years he traveled over much of India, residing for two years at Nalanda.

I-Tsing, whom I have mentioned before, was one of those who followed Hiuen Tsang to India, leaving by sea in 671. After several years of study in Shrivijaya in Sumatra, he reached India and studied at Nalanda during the years A.D. 675 to 685.

This exchange of scholars and of manuscripts continued all through the next several centuries, the connections depending much on the conditions of travel and of occasional warfare between intervening nations. (The scholars were almost always exempt from this, being passed between warring armies with few problems.)

Travel in what has been known as Sinkiang or Chinese Turkestan has never been a simple thing. The Silk Road skirts the Taklamakan Desert on the south along the base of the Kuen-lun Mountains, the second-highest range — and perhaps the least-known — in the world. Another branch follows a northern route through Aksu. Both are usually beset by bandits, and travel is at all times difficult. Sandstorms are common, the desert route has few watering places, and accommodations are primitive by Western standards.

The people are of a variety of nationalities. Only a few are Chinese, of the Han variety; most are of Turkish descent. It is a harsh and haunted land, yet one that can be rarely beautiful, and one that has been crossed and recrossed by scholars seeking wisdom, or at least a better understanding.

Turkestan Down to the Mongol Invasion by W. Bartold proved an excellent book, and I followed it with Howorth's great study of the Mongols in five volumes. I then went on to read Burton Watson's translation of Ssu-ma Ch'ien's *Shih-Chi*, and followed it with Pan-Ku's *History of the Former Han Dynasty*, the oldest histories of China to which we presently have access.

From those first years at home and in the Jamestown Public Library, books have been an adventure. A fast-moving boxcar, what we often called a "side-door Pullman," was as easy a place to read as anywhere else, and I read some good books while en route.

As I have been writing this book, old memories of books read return to me, among them Jack London's *Burning Daylight*, which I read on a bus traveling through Texas, and Gogol's *Taras Bulba*, which I read one bitterly cold night in Paris.

I had come there with a convoy of empty tank trucks to draw gasoline. A few hours before, we had been far up the line and had delivered our gas and turned in. Minutes later, we had been awakened and told to get the hell out of there, that the Germans were attacking. We were on the road within minutes, thus escaping the Battle of the Bulge.

For hours we had waited to gas up and return. The officer in charge of the gas dump was so fearful of saboteurs that he would not open even for us. (As the Germans had begun the strike that culminated in the Battle of the Bulge, they had dropped a number of four-man sabotage teams over the country, most of them equipped with American arms, jeeps, and such. I had captured two men of one such team near the big gas dump at Chartres, but they were in German uniforms.)

Supposedly these were hand-picked men, trained for their jobs, and the officer in command of the dump in Paris had been briefed. The difficulty was that in his case sabotage was not necessary; all the Germans had to do to put the dump out of action was scare him enough. Only at daylight did we finally succeed in convincing him it was safe.

It was bitterly cold that night and each of us made out as best we could, no fires being tolerated so close to the dump. Drivers huddled in the cabs of their trucks, and my driver and I did as well as we could in an enclosed jeep. My driver took over the back seat and, wrapped in his army overcoat, seemed to make out pretty well.

Every now and again I got out of the jeep and walked along my empty tank trucks, just checking. No Germans appeared and I was just as happy to be left alone. Most of the night I read *Taras Bulba* and wished for daylight and, hopefully, a warm sun.

28

When one takes the time to survey the efforts that have been made to preserve man's record on earth, the results are astonishing. Upon consideration, it becomes apparent that this need to leave some account of his presence here has been most important.

His great walls, his pyramids, and his temples are an important but minor aspect, for obviously the most important has been the written word. Man has endeavored by every means possible to explain his being here, where he hopes to go, and how he plans to go about it.

Is this explanation only for himself and his peers? Or does he hope to explain to future generations what he has been, thought, and wondered?

At a quick glance we might accept the idea that men write to themselves, that they ask their questions and pose their replies for others of their kind. But is that all?

It seems to me that every written word is an effort to understand man's place in the universe. What is he? What is he becoming?

Will he populate the infinite number of planets that lie out there waiting? Or has that been done already by other forms of life?

We are, finally, all wanderers in search of knowledge. Most of us hold the dream of becoming something better than we are, something larger, richer, in some way more important to the world and ourselves. Too often, the way taken is the wrong way, with too much emphasis on what we want to have, rather than what we wish to become.

What has been offered here is one man's quest for knowledge, in which he is much less impressed by what he has done than by what has not been done. Along the way I have written some stories — stories for people I have known about people I have known. These stories contain moments of drama because their intent is to entertain, but woven into their lines is much about how men have lived, fought, and survived. The world in which I have lived has often been a harsh, bitter one, but it has always been tinged with romance. I doubt I could have endured the one without the other.

In Sinkiang and the Pamirs, the Taklamakan and some parts of Tibet, when one party meets another on the way, the greeting is often *"May there be a road!"* It is a land of frequent snowslides, rockslides, and cave-ins. Roads are casually made; bridges are usually hanging from ropes, so the saying is apropos: One hopes the way will be clear, the road open. So as one pilgrim to another, I leave you with that wish: "May there be a road!"

Death's a fierce meadowlark: but to die
   having made
Something more equal to the centuries
Than muscle and bone, is mostly to shed
   weakness.
The mountains are dead stone, the people
Admire or hate their stature, their insolent
   quietness,
The mountains are not softened nor troubled
And a few dead men's thoughts have the
   same temper.
> — ROBINSON JEFFERS
> from "Wise Men in Their Bad Hours"

BIBLIOGRAPHY

As I expected to reread parts of these books, I wanted their titles available to me. Hence, I kept this listing of books read from 1930 to 1935 and in 1937.

(Asterisks represent books reviewed for *The Oklahoman*.)

BOOKS AND PLAYS READ IN 1930

1. Three Philosophical Poets, *George Santayana*
2. Winds of Doctrine, *George Santayana*
3. Reason in Society, *George Santayana*
4. Selected Stories, *Joseph Conrad*
5. Soliloquies, *Friedrich Schleiermacher*
6. Tales, Volume II, *Edgar Allan Poe*
7. Romances, Volume II, *Voltaire*
8. Romances, Volume I, *Voltaire*
9. The Hermit of Carmel, *George Santayana*
10. Thus Spake Zarathustra, *Friedrich Nietzsche*
11. Black Sparta, *Naomi Mitchison*
12. The War of the Worlds, *H. G. Wells*
13. Dynamo, *Eugene O'Neill*

114. New Arabian Nights,
Robert Louis Stevenson
115. The Mind of Mischief,
William S. Sadler, M.D.

BOOKS AND PLAYS READ IN 1931

1. The Soul of Lilith, *Marie Corelli*
2. The Passionate Rebel, *Kasimir Edschmid*
3. The Garden of Kama and Other Love Lyrics from India, *Laurence Hope*
4. Songs of the Dead End, *Patrick MacGill*
5. Our Business Civilization, *James Truslow Adams*
6. Iconoclasts, *James Huneker*
7. Brand, *Henrik Ibsen*
8. The Devil's Disciple, *George Bernard Shaw*
9. Plays, *August Strindberg*
10. The Hasîdah, *Haji Abdû El-Yezdi*
11. Poetry, *Algernon Charles Swinburne*
12. Castle Gay, *John Buchan*
13. The Prince, *Niccolò Machiavelli*
14. Against the Grain, *J. K. Huysmans*
15. Cashel Byron's Profession, *George Bernard Shaw*
16. Outline of Abnormal Psychology, *William McDougall*
17. Crime and Punishment, *Fyodor Dostoevsky*
18. The Time Machine, *H. G. Wells*

BOOKS AND PLAYS READ IN 1932

1. Beyond Good and Evil,
   Friedrich Nietzsche
2. Assorted articles, *D. H. Lawrence*
3. Hollyhocks and Goldenglow,
   Elbert Hubbard
4. Charles Baudelaire, *Arthur Symons*
5. Psychotherapy, *Edward W. Taylor*
6. N by E, *Rockwell Kent*
7. The Book of the Damned, *Charles Fort*
8. Bystander, *Maxim Gorky*
9. Success, *Lion Feuchtwanger*
10. A Preface to Morals, *Walter Lippmann*
11. Deluge, *S. Fowler Wright*
12. Lady Chatterley's Lover,
    D. H. Lawrence
13. The Psychology of Mental Disorders,
    Abraham Myerson, M.D.
14. The Art of Thinking, *Ernest Dimnet*
15. Harlem Shadows, *Claude McKay*
16. The Function of Reason,
    Alfred North Whitehead
17. The Psychopathology of Everyday Life,
    Sigmund Freud
18. The Misuse of Mind, *Karin Stephen*
19. Psychology, *Everett Dean Martin*
20. The Philosophy of Style, *Herbert Spencer*
21. Mysticism and Logic, *Bertrand Russell*
22. The Meaning of Culture,
    John Cowper Powys
23. Philosophy, *Nicholas Murray Butler*

49. Poetical Works, *Oscar Wilde*
50. Poetry, *Edgar Allan Poe*
51. Socialism in America, *John Macy*
52. Representative Men,
    Ralph Waldo Emerson
53. On Liberty, *John Stuart Mill*
54. Faust, *Goethe*
55. Essays, *Henry David Thoreau*
56. Lyrics of Lowly Life,
    Paul Laurence Dunbar
57. The Rise of Silas Lapham,
    William Dean Howells
58. Law for the American Farmer,
    John B. Green
59. History of the Intellectual Development
    of Europe, Volume I, *John W. Draper*
60. The Mill on the Floss, *George Eliot*
61. Gillespie, *J. MacDougall Hay*
62. The White Company,
    Arthur Conan Doyle
63. History of the Intellectual Development
    of Europe, Volume II, *John W. Draper*
64. Julius Caesar, *William Shakespeare*
65. As You Like It, *William Shakespeare*
66. The Law of Biogenesis,
    J. Howard Moore
67. Socialism and Philosophy,
    Antonio Labriola
68. The Taming of the Shrew,
    William Shakespeare
69. Dakota, *Edna La Moore Waldo*
70. Josephus, *Lion Feuchtwanger*

BOOKS AND PLAYS READ IN 1933

10. The History of Civilization in England, Volume III, *Henry Buckle*
11. Science and Education, *Thomas H. Huxley*
12. The History of Civilization in England, Volume IV, *Henry Buckle*
13. Lalla Rookh, *Thomas Moore*
14. The History of English Literature, Volume I, *H. A. Taine*
15. The Return of the Native, *Thomas Hardy*
16. The Reign of Law, *James Lane Allen*
17. The Tempest, *William Shakespeare*
18. The History of English Literature, Volume II, *H. A. Taine*
19. The Critic, *Richard Brinsley Sheridan*
20. Timon of Athens, *William Shakespeare*
21. Don Juan, *Lord Byron*
22. Troilus and Cressida, *William Shakespeare*
23. The Origin of Species, *Charles Darwin*
24. The History of English Literature, Volume III, *H. A. Taine*
25. The Admirable Bashville, *George Bernard Shaw*
26. Lady Windermere's Fan, *Oscar Wilde*
27. The Death of the Gods, *Dmitry Merezhkovsky*
28. Man and Technics, *Oswald Spengler*
29. Tono-Bungay, *H. G. Wells*
30. A Doll's House, *Henrik Ibsen*
31. Winesburg, Ohio, *Sherwood Anderson*
32. A House of Gentlefolk, *Ivan Turgenev*
33. David, *D. H. Lawrence*

79. Robert Burns, *John Drinkwater*
80. Elizabeth the Queen, *Maxwell Anderson*
81. Enough Rope, *Dorothy Parker*
82. Poetical Works, *Li Po*
83. Three Essays, *Thomas Mann*
84. Power, *Lion Feuchtwanger*
85. Lord Jim, *Joseph Conrad*
86. Saint Joan, *George Bernard Shaw*
87. Titans of Literature, *Burton Rascoe*
88. This Believing World, *Lewis Browne*
89. I Cover the Waterfront, *Max Miller*
90. The Greek Way, *Edith Hamilton*
91. Candide, *Voltaire*
92. Thirst, *Eugene O'Neill*
93. Since Victor Hugo, *Bernard Fay*
94. Both Your Houses, *Maxwell Anderson*
95. The Best Short Stories of 1933, *Edward J. O'Brien, editor*
96. The Life of Beardsley, *Haldane Macfall*
97. New Russia's Primer, *M. Ilin*
98. Twenty-five Finest Short Stories, *Edward J. O'Brien, editor*
99. Writing for Money, *Sydney Horler*
100. The Heptameron, *Marguerite, Queen of Navarre*
101. Dionysus in Doubt, *Edwin Arlington Robinson*
102. The Age of Reason, *Thomas Paine*
103. The History of English Literature, Volume IV, *H. A. Taine*
104. When Worlds Collide, *Edwin Balmer and Philip Wylie*

105. South Wind, *Norman Douglas*

BOOKS AND PLAYS READ IN 1934

1. The Apple Cart, *George Bernard Shaw*
2. The Lovely Lady, *D. H. Lawrence*
3. Better Writing, *Henry Seidel Canby*
4. Figures of Earth, *James Branch Cabell*
5. Oil for the Lamps of China,
   Alice Tisdale Hobart
6. The Adventures of the Black Girl in Her
   Search for God, *George Bernard Shaw*
7. The Virgin and the Gipsy,
   D. H. Lawrence
8. Our Unconscious Mind, *Frederick Pierce*
9. King Kong, *Edgar Wallace*
10. The Woman of Andros, *Thornton Wilder*
11. Mademoiselle de Maupin,
    Théophile Gautier
12. Manfred, *Lord Byron*
13. Prometheus Bound, *Aeschylus*
14. The Life of Man, *Leonid Andreyev*
15. You Gotta Be Rough,
    Michael Fiaschetti
16. The New American Credo,
    George Jean Nathan
17. Mutiny on the Bounty,
    Charles Nordhoff and James Norman Hall
18. Command, *William McFee*
19. Victory, *Joseph Conrad*
20. Man and Mask, *Feodor Chaliapin*

351

106. The Tale of a Shipwreck,
    James Norman Hall
107. The Foundry, *Albert Halper*
108. The Son of Man, *Emil Ludwig*
109. Man Possessed, *William Rose Benét*
110. The Testaments, *François Villon*
111. Contemporary Poetry,
    Marguerite Wilkinson
112. The Morbid Personality, *Sandor Lorand*
113. Hamlet, *William Shakespeare*
114. Henry VI, Part I, *William Shakespeare*

BOOKS AND PLAYS READ IN 1935

1. Henry VI, Part II, *William Shakespeare*
2. Riker of the Seven Seas,
    Frederic H. Riker
3. South of the Sun, *Russell Owen★*
4. The Search for the Northwest Passage,
    Nellis M. Crouse★
5. This Wanderer, *Louis Golding★*
6. The Abbey of Evolayne, *Paule Regnier★*
7. Highland Night, *Neil M. Gunn★*
8. Israfel, *Hervey Allen★*
9. Pylon, *William Faulkner★*
10. The Pumpkin Coach, *Louis Paul★*
11. While Rome Burns, *Alexander Woollcott*
12. The Klondyke Nugget,
    Russell A. Bankson★
13. Talk United States!, *Robert Whitcomb★*
14. Henry VI, Part III, *William Shakespeare*

63. The "Johanna Maria",
    *Arthur Van Schendel**
64. Marco Millions, *Eugene O'Neill*
65. The Story of the Human Race,
    *Henry Thomas**
66. The Tempest, *William Shakespeare*
67. Racing the Seas, *Walter and Olson**
68. European Experiences,
    *Mabel Dodge Luhan**
69. The Seas Were Mine,
    *Captain Howard Hartman**
70. Level Land, *Kenneth C. Kaufman**
71. Design for Living, *Noël Coward*
72. Pink Pants, *Holton and Balliol**
73. The Wild Duck, *Henrik Ibsen*

BOOKS AND PLAYS READ IN 1937

1. Genghis Khan, *Harold Lamb*
2. Reasons for Anger, *Robert Briffault**
3. Song for a Listener, *Leonard Feeney**
4. Buckboard Days, *Sophie A. Poe**
5. First Men in the Moon, *H. G. Wells*
6. Westward from Rio,
    Bowman and Dickinson
7. Forgotten Towns of Southern New Jersey,
    *Henry C. Beck**
8. Unequal to Song, *Charles Martin**
9. Tamerlane, *Harold Lamb*
10. More Than Bread, *Joseph Auslander**
11. Deserts on the March, *Paul B. Sears*